SECURITIES

- What They Are
- Their Markets
- Regulations
- Analysis
- Financial Planning

by Raymond H. Jacobs

Volume 2 FINANCIAL PLANNING AND MUTUAL FUNDS

SECOND EDITION

PUBLISHED BY KALB, VOORHIS & CO.

OTHER KALB, VOORHIS PUBLICATIONS:

- The Financial Planning Study Series
- How to Make Your Money Work for You, Your Wife, Your Children
- KV Convertible Fact-Finder
- The Convertible Bond Handbook

(For investment dealers only)
- The Financial Planning Workbook
- KV Mutual Fund Reports
- The Pocket Summary of Mutual Funds
- Current Data (Mutual Funds)

Table of Contents

1 FINANCIAL PLANNING

GENERAL CONSIDERATIONS   2 1
>   (*What financial planning is, why important*)
>   A Healthy Financial Program
>   *Life insurance, emergency fund, investments*
>   Life Insurance
>   *How much to carry*
>   Emergency Fund
>   *Its importance*
>   Investments
>   *Both fixed and variable needed*

INVESTMENT COMPANIES   2–5
>   Closed-End and Open-End Funds
>   *Comparison; leveraged companies*

VARIABLE ANNUITIES   2–7
>   The Theory of Annuity
>   *Fixed annuity, non-refund and certain annuities*
>   Fixed Annuities: Advantages and Disadvantages
>   *Their safety; but static investments, no inflation hedge*
>   The Variable Annuity Concept
>   *How it differs from fixed annuity*

CONTENTS

The Two Types of Variable Annuity Units
Accumulation and annuity

Variations

REAL ESTATE INVESTMENT TRUSTS   2–11
    Background
       Real estate syndicates and corporations
    Legal Requirements
       Authorized by 1960 law

MONTHLY INVESTMENT PLAN   2–12
    (Of the New York Stock Exchange)

A BRIEF COMPARISON WITH MUTUAL FUNDS   2–13
    Variable Annuities
    Real Estate Investment Trusts
    The MIP

THE KEOGH ACT   2–14
    (Self-Employed Individuals Retirement Act of 1962)

TAXES   2–15
    Income Taxes
       Federal tax highlights, treatments of capital gains and losses
    Corporate Taxes
       On net profits, dividends
    Property Taxes
    Estate and Inheritance Taxes
       Federal and state, necessity of legal advice
    Gift Taxes
       Lifetime gift exemption, annual exclusion, gifts in anticipation of death, gifts to minors

REGISTRATION OF SECURITIES   2–21

THE REGISTERED REPRESENTATIVE   2–25
    Unauthorized Practice of Law
    Regulation of Credit
       Loans by Brokers, loans by banks

CONTENTS

2 MUTUAL FUNDS

BACKGROUND   2–29
(The concept of spreading risk)
Development
Why investment companies grew
Modern Investment Companies
Growth during 1920's, "mutual funds," Federal regulation and Act of 1940, reasons for recent growth

OBJECTIVES AND CLASSIFICATION   2–32
Fund Objectives
Measuring the success of a fund
Classification by Objective
Stability of capital or conservation of principal, income, growth
Classification by Portfolio
Five types—bond, and preferred stock, balanced, common stock, industry
Classification by Management Type
Restricted, fully managed

SOME BASIC FACTS   2–35
The Purchase of Shares
As an outright purchase, accumulation plan, dividend reinvestment plan, withdrawal plan
Income Dividends and Capital Gains
How they are derived
Sales Charge
Letter of intent, rights of accumulation
Is There a Typical Investor?
The "average" investor

MUTUAL FUNDS AND TAXES   2–37
"Regulated Investment Companies"
Tax Treatment
The Shareholder's Tax Liability
Capital gains and dividends

3 ORGANIZATION OF MUTUAL FUNDS

STRUCTURE   2–41
Fund Personnel
Directors, officers, clerical

CONTENTS

Management
> *The management company, fee*

Underwriter
> *Function, fee*

The Custodian
> *Safekeeping of cash and securities*

Transfer Agent
> *For issuance and cancellation of shares*

A Fund as a Trust
> *As a trust instead of a corporation*

EXCHANGE-TYPE FUNDS   2–47
(Developed to relieve tax problem)

Background
> *Basis under Internal Revenue Code*

Exchange Procedure

Cost Base
> *How cost carried over to Fund shares*

Taxes
> *Capital gains, unrealized losses*

Redemption
> *Cash or "in kind"*

4 THE INVESTMENT COMPANY ACT OF 1940

A CHARTER FOR THE MUTUAL FUND INDUSTRY   2–53
(Why proposed, basic intent, highlights)

PROVISIONS OF THE ACT   2–54
(Summary of its 53 sections)

5 THE MUTUAL FUND PROSPECTUS   2–67

ITS IMPORTANCE TO THE INVESTOR   2–67
(A requirement for "full and fair disclosure," SEC standards)

PAGE ONE   2–68
No SEC Approval
> *Of the securities themselves*

Offering Price
> *How determined*

Contents

CONTENTS

Objectives and Methods
   Of the particular fund

"No Assurance . . ."
   That objective will be met

THE COMPANY AND ITS POLICIES   2–70

Type of Company

Policies and Restrictions
   Of the fund itself, imposed by Act of 1940

Distributions
   Policy on dividends and security profits

Offering Price Computation
   How shares are bought and sold, "break-point" sales

CHANGES IN SHARE VALUE   2–74

"Per Share Income and Capital Changes"
   Table of income and expense and of operating expenses to income

Redemption or Repurchase
   How liquidating value is determined

GENERAL INFORMATION   2–78

Fund Management
   Terms of management agreement

Principal Underwriter
   Agreement, expenses

Officers and Directors
   Their experience and affiliations

General Information
   Date of Incorporation, officers' holdings

The Custodian
   Limitations of his role

SPECIAL FEATURES   2–79

1. Income Plan
   Outright purchase of shares

2. Dividend Reinvestment Plan
   Reinvestment of capital gains and dividends

3. Accumulation Plans
   Specifications of voluntary accumulation plans

4. Open Account
   Additional purchase at investor's option

5. Withdrawal Plan
   Fixed share or fixed dollar withdrawals

Illustrations of Assumed Investments
   Results shown in tabular and/or chart form

FINANCIAL STATEMENTS   2–82

Schedule of Investments
   The portfolio of securities

Assets and Liabilities
   Typical balance sheet

Income and Expense
   *Arriving at net income, gain on investments, unrealized
   appreciation or depreciation*

Changes in Net Assets
   Year-to-year change

Auditor's Report

Officers

Omitted Information
   Non-essential information

The Self-Employed Retirement Act
   If fund offers shares under Keogh Act

6   **THE STATEMENT OF POLICY**

ITS PURPOSE   2–93

(*What may, may not, and must be stated in marketing fund shares*)

HOW IT IS USED   2–93

(*A guide to representatives, definition of 'literature'*)

Sales Literature Defined
   'Any communication'

"Materially Misleading . . ."
   Violating fraud section of the '33 Act

"What is Fund X's Rate of Return?"
   Implying a percentage return

Presentation of Distributions
   Separating capital gains and income distributions

Misrepresenting the Return
   Implying a set return

CONTENTS

Implying Preservation or Gain of Capital
Importance of explanation of inherent market risks

Federal Registration Explained
Registration is not supervision

The Custodian's Function
No more than physical possession of assets

How Much Are Shares Worth at Redemption?
More or less than cost

Comparing a Fund with a Debt Security
Not a debt-type security

Comparing with Another Security . . . or Investment . . . or
Index or Average
Difficulty of a fair comparison, home-made comparisons, making it clear

Funds are not "New Capital" for Industry
Already-issued securities do not create "new capital"

Performance Charts and Tables
All fund charts are substantially the same

The Correct Word for Management
No "extravagant" claims

A Fund is Not a Cooperative
Many points of difference

Fiduciaries and Investment Companies
Funds are not "selected" by fiduciaries

Dollar-Cost-Averaging
Necessity of clear explanation

The Sales Charge
"A clear reference"

Switching a Security
The cost involved

Comparing Fund Performance with Industry Performance
Cannot be measured or compared

Use of Other Published Material
Only when it complies with SOP and is not out of context

CONTRACTUAL PLANS

INTRODUCTION   2–115
Definition
An accumulation plan with a definite goal

History
> *Recent growth, completion records*

Features
> *Definite goal, incentive, insurance, guaranteed charges, reinvestment at NAV, possible lower sales charge, partial liquidation, tax savings*

THE PLAN PROSPECTUS   2–120

Page One
> *Explanation of charges and types of plans*

No SEC Approval
> *Must be accompanied by fund prospectus*

Table of Contents

The Plans
> *Single payment and systematic investment plans*

Charts
> *Distribution of charges, single payment plans, insurance costs*

Rights and Privileges
> *Dividends, beneficiary, partial wtihdrawals, transfer, termination, receipts and reports, default and reinstatement, meetings and voting rights, advance payments*

Sales and Service Charges

Plan Completion Insurance

Tax Status

Underlying Fund

Monthly Withdrawal Plans

Substitution of Shares
> *Changing to another fund or investment*

GENERAL INFORMATION   2–128

Custodian
> *Requirements and duties*

Sponsor (The Plan Company)
> *Basic information*

General
> *How plans are sold, miscellaneous information*

Hypotheticals
> *Tables of assumed investments*

CONTENTS

Financial Statements

Application Forms

8 WITHDRAWAL PLANS

BACKGROUND   2–133

    Definition
        A planned withdrawal of dollars or shares, problem of capital invasion

    Flexibility
        Variable dollar or equal dollar payments, adjusting to life expectancy

    Inherent Risks
        Plans are not a method of conserving capital

THE WITHDRAWAL PLAN FOLDER   2–135

    Features
        Budgeting, planned distribution, capital growth, reporting non-forfeiture, adding additional sums, charges and fees

    The Table of Assumed Payments
        Hypothetical programs, qualifications as to payment results

THE TAX CONSEQUENCE   2–139

    Income and Capital Gains
        Basis of liquidation—FIFO, LIFO, or identified shares

    Wash Sales
        Acquiring "substantially identical" securities

INDEX   2–143

Chapter 1

Financial Planning

GENERAL CONSIDERATIONS

Financial planning is the art of dealing with an individual's financial objectives during his lifetime so that his present and future needs are satisfied as far as possible within his monetary limits and so that his property at death is efficiently and properly arranged.

Many factors must be taken into account: current income; savings and property; income over the years; the possibility of accumulating additional property; college expenses for children; retirement; and adequate provision for the family after the breadwinner's death—whether the death comes prematurely or at an advanced age.

It is a truism that a firm foundation for the future can be laid only by proper planning during the present. Yet there are many who plan inadequately because they do not seek the advice of specialists in the complicated fields of life insurance, retirement, pension plans, forms of property ownership, wills and intestacy, trusts, and estate transfer problems.

Even a person who does not own a large amount of property or other assets should be concerned with his complete financial picture. He should be aware of the benefits of life insurance and social security. He should have a cash reserve for emergencies. He should have a plan to accumulate capital for the future which will not conflict with his current needs.

A Healthy Financial Program

The head of a family may have a variety of business or personal reasons for capital accumulation. But whatever his reasons, he has the double obligation to support his family and himself during his lifetime and to care for them after his death. For a healthy financial program he needs:

Adequate life insurance. The primary purpose of life insurance is to ensure the financial well-being of the insured's dependents should he die too soon. On his death, life insurance creates an immediate estate that he may not have had time enough to accumulate during his lifetime. For the young married man, just starting out on his career, there is probably no other way to meet this obligation.

An emergency fund. This is not a cash reserve for foreseen needs, but for the unforeseen. It should be excluded from consideration for use other than in actual emergencies. In no sense, should the emergency fund be considered as a specific part of an investment program.

Investments. After present living expenses are taken care of, the average person is left with some extra dollars which can be used to accumulate more dollars for specific future income needs. Depending on his circumstances, some investments should probably be geared to producing future income. Other investments should be for possible long-term growth and variable future income.

Life Insurance

There are a very few people who do not need life insurance. An unmarried man just beginning a career may be needlessly encumbered if he purchases life insurance before he knows the type of future obligations he must face. A man or woman alone in life, with no present or expected dependents, may be better advised to find another use for his money. The after-tax estate of some wealthy people amply provide for dependents; such people may not need life insurance.

However, most working men have a wife, children, and often parents who are primarily dependent on his salary. While the family may be well provided for during the wage earner's life, it is a statistic that comparatively few are as well provided for after the wage earner's death. In the United States, with an average family income exceeding $7500 a year, the average life insurance carried by all *insured* families is $14,300—or less than the equivalent of two years' pay. And since a significant minority of all families carry no life insurance whatsoever, the average family, including all the uninsured, carries a total of $11,400.*

Life insurance proceeds must often be used to pay medical and hospital bills incurred for illness before death as well as the cost of burial. Even with Social Security benefits, pensions, and other income sources a widow with or without children is all too often forced to adapt to a pitifully declined standard of living.

---

* From statistics for 1962 compiled by the Life Insurance Association of America.

How much life insurance should a man carry? There is no easy answer. Although each case must be studied on its individual needs, it is a fair assumption that a man would like to leave enough so that his survivors' standard of living after his death is not reduced. He must take into account:

- The decreased number in the family.
- The amounts and duration of Social Security benefits.
- Company or other pensions.
- Reduced taxes (certain types of income will be tax-exempt).
- Mortgage insurance on his home. This can greatly reduce family living costs or else provide a cash sum.
- Any other income from investments or business interests.

With all factors taken into consideration, a man should carry enough life insurance so that the income the family can derive from it and from other capital resources will maintain the desired standard of living. How the income is derived depends on the employment of the insurance proceeds and other capital. Guaranteed insurance annuities alone (or annuity options) will produce one figure. Quite different (and possibly varying) results will accrue from a combination of annuities and lump sum investments in securities.

What kind of insurance? There are many variations tailored to suit individual preferences, and even with all the facts and figures it is often difficult to ascertain which is the best for each person.

Most life insurance salesman will recommend ordinary or "whole" life insurance in preference to term insurance. For a young wage earner with a growing family who cannot afford the premium for whole life, but who must nevertheless provide adequate insurance, an insurance salesman might recommend a certain minimum of ordinary life with supplemental term insurance. The mathematics of insurance can become complex, and only a qualified insurance man can be said to understand and to be able to explain the advantages of the different types of insurance.

Emergency Fund

The ready money needed in an emergency fund should be in an easily accessible form. Cash, savings accounts, and savings bonds are the basis of most emergency funds. Experts differ regarding the amount required for an emergency fund, but the consensus seems to be the equivalent of six months' take-home pay. While sickness and accident insurance might seem to take the place of at least part of the fund, it will not provide against the loss of a job or the loss of a business.

Both an adequate emergency fund and adequate insurance are required before any investment program should be started. People who do not have an emergency fund are usually among those who need it the most and who are most likely to be "wiped out" in a sudden financial crisis. Equity investments by such people would be unwise because, in an emergency, they may be forced to liquidate at a loss.

Investments

The financial picture for future years must be planned . . . both for future working years and for future years of retirement. All too often the retired find that fixed pensions and annuities must be stretched farther each year to fit the rising cost of living. Because of the varying buying power of the dollar, hedges must be provided against inflation as well as the possibility of deflation.

The fixed-income dollar, which comes from fixed annuities and pensions and, in some degree, from Social Security payments, is necessary as a deflation hedge. If the purchasing power of the dollar rises, a fixed income becomes more valuable. If the purchasing power of the dollar decreases—as inflation gains—the income from equities has a good chance of increasing and offsetting the rise. The advantage of the fixed-dollar deflation hedge is that the dollar is always there; the variable dollar inflation hedge is not certain, but investments that can grow with the cost of living give the only possibility of an inflation hedge.

Let us say that half of the retirement dollar should provide a fixed return, and the other half a variable return. The fixed portion could then include Social Security benefits or other fixed pensions and retirement annuities. The other half should then include investments in such forms as variable annuities, equities in stocks, or other securities.

For most people who depend on regular paychecks, the best way to save for retirement is through a regular investment program. Each case, of course, is individual and the importance of professional advice cannot be stressed too strongly.

Here is one example of the need for balance in an investment program.

Suppose a man bought an insurance annuity in 1928. Payments of $100 a month from the annuity started immediately. For approximately the same amount of money, he purchased a representative cross-section of common stocks that also immediately produced dividends at the same rate ($100 a month). (Commissions are excluded for this hypothetical purchase.)

Now, had such a representative unsupervised portfolio of stocks performed in the same manner as the Standard and Poor's 500-stock index, the *combined purchasing power* from the stocks and annuity in terms of 1928 dollars would never have varied in the next 30 years by more than 15 per cent from $200 in any one month. The average combined purchasing power for 30 years would have been within five per cent of the $200 per month he received in 1928.

It so happens that the proportion between annuity value and stock value in 1928 was about 50-50 in order to produce these results. Even though the ratio would vary yearly because of changing average stock dividends, the principle remains the same. Both variable and fixed dollars are needed to achieve balance in purchasing power.

Thus equity investment is part of a well-rounded financial program. When properly applied it takes its place along with life insurance and the required emergency fund for the satisfaction of financial goals. However, it must be emphasized that a program for acquiring equity investments should be undertaken only by those individuals with job security, adequate life insurance, and adequate emergency funds. Also, a periodic review should be made for possible increased needs for insurance and emergencies that occur as a result of increased income.

The decision as to the type of investment program can be made only by the investor himself. Professional guidance is available through qualified insurance agents, securities dealers, accountants and attorneys.

There are several investment methods for providing variable dollar income. Discussed in the following pages are *investment companies*, of which there are several types; *variable annuities*, which are marketed by a few life insurance companies as part of a retirement program; *real estate investment trusts*; the *monthly investment plan* of the New York Stock Exchange, and the *Self-Employed Individuals Tax Retirement Act of 1962* (known as the Keogh Act).

INVESTMENT COMPANIES

Closed-End and Open-End Funds

Investment companies manage the collective money of the individuals and institutions who invest in them. Because investment companies are organized to pursue any one of a variety of objectives—growth of capital, income, safety, etc.—investors can choose the company which appears most suited to their needs.

The two broad types of investment companies, *closed-end* and *open-end* (*mutual funds*), are organized under provisions of the Investment Company Act of 1940 (see Chapter 4). They both provide the professional planning required for a workable investment program. They also offer the advantages of investment diversification and convenience.

The basic difference between the two is in their capitalization.

The closed-end company issues a fixed number of shares as does any other type of corporation. After the issue has been bought by the public, the shares are traded over-the-counter or on an exchange, or both. The issuing company does not continuously issue shares, nor will it redeem its own outstanding shares. Because of the manner in which the shares are traded, the shares of closed-end companies frequently sell at a price greater than their net asset value ("at a premium") or at a price below the actual net asset value ("at a discount").

An open-end investment company issues shares continuously to new buyers and stands ready to redeem its own shares at any time. The company *must* receive the actual net asset value per share for the new shares it issues to prevent any change in relative value in the other shares outstanding. When the company redeems shares, it pays the holder the actual net asset value per share. Sometimes, but rarely, it deducts a small liquidating fee.

There are some funds that are open-end only at one end, that is, they have issued a number of shares and will not issue any more. However, unlike the closed-end company, they will redeem their outstanding shares at net asset value at any time.

There are other differences and similarities between the two types of funds.

While open-end funds have only one type of share, closed-end funds may also have warrants or senior securities outstanding in addition to their regular shares.

Some closed-end funds have two classes of shares . . . "income" and "capital." The income shares offered by these "leveraged" or "dual" funds amount to a type of preferred stock with a specified minimum rate of return. The capital shares offer no yield but give the investors two-fold capital appreciation possibilities. Equal dollar amounts of both types of shares are issued. All income from the entire fund accrues and is paid to the income shareholders, after deduction of expenses. Redeemable at a stated time or on notice after a stated time, the income shares do not share in any capital growth of the fund. Holders of the capital or common shares receive no income, but share in the growth or depreciation of the entire fund. Thus, both types of shares are "leveraged." The income shareholders benefit from the income from twice their investment; the capital shareholders benefit from or lose the entire change in the value of the portfolio. Unless the value of the portfolio (comprising all of the assets of the entire fund) were to drop fifty per cent or more, the preferred shareholders are assured at least the value of their investment . . . they would be in a loss position only were the combined assets of the fund to drop below the fifty per cent mark. On the other hand, any increase or decrease in value of the fund as a whole has a double effect on the net asset value per share of the capital shares. Shares of the fund are not redeemable until the preferred shares are called for redemption. At that time, the preferred shareholders can take the stipulated value of their shares in cash or exchange them without sales charge for capital shares based on the then net asset value of the capital shares. After redemption of the preferred shares, the fund becomes an open-end fund. Prior to that time, both classes of shares may be traded either on an exchange or over the counter and may, of course, sell at a premium or discount. During its closed-end period, realized long-term capital gains are not distributed. They are retained, with taxes being paid by the fund directly at the maximum long-term capital gains tax rate. The gains and taxes are reported to the owners of the capital shares, who declare the capital gains on their own returns and take a tax credit for the taxes paid by the fund. Such reported gains add to the cost basis of the capital shares.

There is a wide spectrum of closed-end funds. Some are widely diversified. Others invest only in particular industries or special situations. Certain funds have wide interests—perhaps controlling interests—in corporations in which they have invested heavily. In such cases, the funds play a part in directing the activities of the company and are not, strictly speaking, simply the managers of other people's money.

The shares of almost all mutual funds can be purchased on a regular investment plan. Shares of some closed-end companies may also be purchased through the monthly investment plan of the New York Stock Exchange.

Also considered as closed-end funds are the *Small Business Investment Companies* (SBIC's) which were made possible by special congressional legislation in 1958. The purpose has been to aid the founding and development of small businesses. Their shares are traded publicly.

VARIABLE ANNUITIES

The Theory of Annuity

A conventional annuity, known as a *fixed annuity*, is traditionally a contract issued by a life insurance company which pays the owner, called the *annuitant*, a specified, guaranteed income for a given number of years or for life when the annuity matures. The following section, a discussion on fixed life annuities, is necessary for comparison purposes with variable annuities.

A life annuity is designed to distribute the *principal* sum invested, together with interest earned, over the annuitant's lifetime.

The table below, which has been used by life insurance companies, will help to explain what annuities are and how they work.

Age at Which Annuity Begins	Monthly Annuity Purchased with $1,000
35	$3.02
40	3.29
45	3.63
50	4.06
55	4.62
60	5.34
65	6.29
70	7.56

These annuities are known as *non-refund* annuities. Payments continue for the lifetime of the annuitant, *no matter how long he lives*, but cease with his death. Even if he were to die after only one payment had been made, no further distribution would be made to his heirs or estate.

There are other annuity forms which guarantee payments for a certain period of time. Known as "10-year certain," "20-year certain," and the like, they guarantee the repayment of part or all of the purchase price even if the annuitant dies before he has collected it himself. These annuities, however, pay less per month than the amounts paid by a non-refund annuity.

The table shows that the age at which the annuity begins is a major factor in determining how much the annuity will be. Mortality tables are used to determine the life expectancy at different ages. The annuity is then based on the expected life of the annuitant, the interest earned by the money held by the life insurance company, and the expenses (including sales charge) charged against the investment. (Life expectancies are generally greater for women than for men and different tables are used.)

Few annuitants live the exact number of years and months predicted by the mortality tables. Some live longer, some do not live as long. Thus, the life insurance companies must deal with averages. The success of their business depends on pooling the risk among a large number of annuitants so that the payments to those who live longer than the average will be compensated for by payments that need not be made to those who die prematurely. In annuities in which a guaranteed payment period is involved, reduced annuity payments are used to offset the time guarantee.

Fixed Annuities: Advantages and Disadvantages

Why do people buy annuities? The advantages are these:
- They provide monthly checks (of part income and part principal) that cannot be outlived.
- They assure *dollar* safety.
- They provide freedom from investment worry.

- They provide a substantially greater dollar flow at certain ages than can be secured on an interest-only basis from conservative individual investments.

The disadvantages of fixed annuities led to the variable annuity. These disadvantages are:

- They are static investments in a dynamic economy. They do not offer the substantial income that can be enjoyed from some other forms of investment.
- As *debt-type* investments, they offer no hedge against inflation.

That the second is the more serious disadvantage is pointed up by the following extract from the State of Wisconsin Study Commission Final Report on Variable Annuities:

The most serious shortcoming of the traditional pension or retirement plan is that it pays the beneficiary only a fixed number of dollars per month, regardless of changes in the purchasing power of the dollar. This defect is inherent in any funded plan in which the accumulated contributions are invested in bonds or other obligations to pay a fixed number of dollars. Since the dollar has declined in buying power for generations, save for a few exceptional periods, the result is that retired persons have suffered severe hardships. Those who have retired in the past decade, for instance, have seen the buying power of their annuity dollars reduced to half what it was when the dollars were contributed to the retirement fund.

Life insurance companies, because of their fixed dollar commitments, are severely restricted as to the types of investments they may make. The vast bulk of their money must be invested in senior securities or other debt-type investments. They must have guarantees in order to meet guarantees. Therefore, even though an insurance company might admit the need for a variable annuity to meet changing economic conditions, there was no way in which such a plan could be set up under the usual investment restrictions placed on the company. This led to the formation of a new type of insurance concept based on the changing value of the dollar called the *variable annuity*.

The Variable Annuity Concept

The traditional annuity guarantees the lifetime payment of a fixed number of dollars every month. The variable annuity guarantees the lifetime payment of the fluctuating value of a fixed number of units every month.

Alternatively, the traditional annuity guarantees the payment of a fixed number of dollars monthly for a specified number of years (e.g. 10-year certain) at a rate somewhat less than that of the non-refund annuity. The variable annuity, on a similar basis, guarantees the payment of the fluctuating value of a fixed number of units monthly for a specified number of years. The number of units is somewhat less than the number of a straight lifetime annuity.

The amount of the monthly payment from a traditional annuity is based on the amount invested, the life expectancy of the annuitant, and a guaranteed interest rate. The number of units, the value of which is to be paid monthly, in a variable annuity is based on the value of accumulated investments, the life expectancy of the annuitant, and the combined income from and change in value of a portfolio of securities.

The Two Types of Variable Annuity Units

There are two types of units, *accumulation* units and *annuity* units.

During the accumulation period, the accumulation units are purchased at their then value, after a deduction for charges, by a fixed monthly payment. The value of these accumulation units is determined by the total worth of the investment portfolio and the total number of units outstanding. During the years that the annuity is being purchased, all dividends, interest, and realized profits are retained in the portfolio itself, thus increasing the value of each unit without adding to the number of previously bought units. Such retained earnings and security profits are not currently taxable to the policyholder when the variable annuity is classified as a life insurance company. The value of a unit may decrease, of course, when the value of portfolio securities decreases during falling markets.

At the end of the accumulation period, the value of the accumulated units is computed. From this value and the mortality table used by the company, the worth of the annuity units is now computed. The company then guarantees to pay the investor the value of that number of units every month for life. Since it depends on the value of the annuity units at the time each check is drawn, the amount of each monthly check will vary.

Variations

While the principles upon which they all operate are similar, the details of different variable annuities differ. All variable annuities must be registered under the Investment Company Act of 1940 as investment companies (by decision of the Supreme Court). However, not all variable annuity companies may *elect* to be treated as insurance companies. Details of accumulation units, annuity units and methods of determining payout vary. Full information regarding any particular variable annuity can be found in its prospectus.

REAL ESTATE INVESTMENT TRUSTS

Background

To many people, investment in real estate is the most desirable of all investments. They seem to get a sense of ownership from real estate that they do not get from shares of stock. However, the feeling of ownership is not the only advantage of real estate investments. Because the Federal government allows depreciation (frequently at an accelerated rate) on improved real estate as a credit against income, the normally high returns (often eight per cent to ten per cent) are often tax free.

Desirable buildings, shopping centers and the like are high-priced items. Few investors have the money or knowledge needed to buy or to build such desirable properties. Also, few individuals are qualified to select management to operate the properties.

To give investors an opportunity to buy such properties, and to obtain money for investment by the originators, the *real estate syndicate* was formed. This is a limited partnership type of company in which the ones who originally form the syndicate are the only general partners. Each public investor is actually a limited partner with typical investments in units of $500, $1,000, $2,000 or more. These syndicates are not subject to Federal income tax at the partnership level. Income received by each of the limited partners is, of course, taxable—except that the depreciation write-off mentioned earlier sometimes results in tax-free income in the early years. Then, if the property is sold by the syndicate at a profit, the investor gets his money back plus a profit that is taxable at long-term capital gain rates.

Such syndicates have several disadvantages. The degree of risk involved varies widely and it is not easy for a prospective investor to determine just what the risk is. This is a management risk over and above the risk inherent in an investment in any real estate. Partnerships are comparatively high-priced for anyone who wishes to invest periodic sums over a period of time. Even in successful operations, the limited partnerships do not have the liquidity of common stocks or other securities. Offerings are relatively infrequent.

There are some corporations that deal primarily in real estate and real estate mortgages. However, these have the disadvantage to the stockholder of having the high Federal corporate income tax applied to net income before distributions of dividends. Because of high depreciation rates, some of these corporations do manage to avoid Federal taxes, but the possibility of doing so decreases with the passage of time. These corporate entities do have the advantages of greater diversification, greater liquidity, and greater ease of purchase in small amounts. Again, the risk is somewhat difficult to evaluate.

The principal *disadvantage* of the corporate real estate company is in its tax treatment. It was to eliminate this disadvantage that the Congress was asked to pass legislation authorizing *real estate investment trusts* corresponding, in some degree, to investment companies. (The Investment Company Act of 1940 expressly disqualified any company whose major business was investing in real estate or real estate mortgages from becoming an investment company.)

Legal Requirements

Public Law 86-779 was passed in 1960 authorizing the new trusts. Under this law, trusts could be formed that had the advantages of the corporate type of company without the disadvantage of the corporate income tax. However, certain requirements must be met by such a trust:

- It must be an unincorporated trust or association, managed by trustees.
- It must have transferable shares or certificates of beneficial interest.
- To qualify for tax exemption, there must be at least 100 owners (either directly or of beneficial interest).
- No five persons may own, directly or indirectly, more than 50 per cent of the beneficial interests.
- Income must be derived in stated minimum percentages from certain sources and in addition at least 75 per cent of total income must be derived from real property.
- At least 90 per cent of income must be distributed to shareholders.
- Realized capital gains will not be taxed to the trust, if distributed to the shareholders . . . if not distributed, they will be taxable to the trust at capital gains rates.
- There must be dissociation of management from the trustees, and the ownership of the trust by management is limited.

MONTHLY INVESTMENT PLAN

For the past several years, a method of buying stocks known as the Monthly Investment Plan (MIP) has been available to the public. Through a member firm of the N.Y. Stock Exchange, an individual can invest as little as $40 a quarter or as much as $1,000 per month towards the purchase of securities listed on the New York Stock Exchange.

After each payment, the investor is credited with a number of shares including a fractional share to the third decimal place of the security or securities he is purchasing. He pays the odd-lot price plus a commission of six per cent for amounts under $100 and for reinvestment of dividends if desired. For investments over $100, the commission is less because it is figured on the same basis as any outright purchase of odd lots. Should he later desire to sell his accumulated shares, he pays a commission on the sale that is related to the number of shares, the dollar amount, and whether or not it is an odd-lot.

By maintaining a regular investment program, the investor will be able to make use of the principle of *dollar-cost-averaging* (Volume 1.)

A BRIEF COMPARISON WITH MUTUAL FUNDS

Variable Annuities

In some respects, the variable annuity plan is similar to plans offered by mutual funds, where the investor acquires shares at regular intervals through fixed payments in an accumulation plan. The accumulation of mutual fund shares is then followed by a withdrawal plan, where the investor regularly withdraws a fixed amount of dollars (or a varying dollar amount through liquidation of equal shares) from interest and capital.

There are some major differences between the two plans.

The variable annuity policyholder has no control over the amount of monthly payment he receives. He is, however, guaranteed payment as long as he lives. The mutual fund shareholder can vary the amount of the payments he receives from a withdrawal plan, although he must be careful not to make the amounts too great. It is possible that large regular withdrawals could exhaust the principal.

Because of the "pooled risk" through the use of mortality tables, the total payout through a variable annuity when the annuitant lives more than 20 years may be considerably more than could be drawn from an equivalent investment in fund shares, if all other factors such as investment performance are the same. This means, of course, that some annuitants forfeit payments through premature death. The shares not withdrawn from an individual's mutual fund account belong to his heirs.

Total charges for the accumulation of units in a life insurance variable annuity are higher than charges for buying mutual fund shares. Over a long-enough period this is offset by the Federal income tax savings on earnings and security profits during the accumulation period of fund shares.

Real Estate Investment Trusts

This form of a trust has certain advantages and disadvantages. While there is a very real possibility of tax-free income and low-taxed capital gains for several years, there is a corresponding chance of capital loss if properties lose income because of a decrease in tenancies or if properties so decline in value that a capital loss is inevitable. Nevertheless the trust does offer professional management and diversification, although the diversification is in one industry and hence considerably more limited than in most mutual funds.

Unlike the dividends from mutual funds, dividends from real estate trusts are not eligible for the current $100 exclusion from the Federal income tax.

Because the trust is not "open-end" in the sense that shares can be redeemed on demand as with a mutual fund, a shareholder could easily experience difficulty in liquidating his holdings in a trust which has all or most of its capital invested.

The MIP

The major distinction between the MIP method of purchase and systematic investment in mutual fund shares is in *what* is being purchased. Through MIP, the investor buys shares of a single or a few corporations. Through a series of periodic investments in mutual fund shares, the investor buys part ownership of a broad portfolio and engages professional managers. This is also done through MIP by the systematic purchase of shares of closed-end investment companies.

One of the great advantages of either program is dollar-cost-averaging (Volume 1.)

THE KEOGH ACT

In 1962 Congress passed the Self-Employed Individuals Tax Retirement Act of 1962, now commonly known as "H.R. 10" or "Keogh." It was amended and liberalized in 1966, with most changes effective as of Jan. 1, 1968. The purpose of this Act was to eliminate the then present inequitable situation between corporate owner-managers and their counterparts self-employed in business and the professions under the business form of a sole-proprietorship or partnership. Previously these persons were not treated as employees and hence were not eligible under the Internal Revenue Code to participate in qualified pension and profit sharing plans.

Under the Keogh Act, a self-employed person is allowed to establish a retirement plan for himself under a tax shelter. However, this plan is still subject to numerous restrictions and does not effectively place the self-employed person on an equal level with employees of corporations. Basically, an individual can set aside each year up to $2,500 or 10% of earned income, whichever is less.

This total amount set aside then qualifies as a deduction in computing Federal income tax liability (for years prior to Jan. 1, 1968 only 50% qualifies). Full time employees, working on a non-seasonal basis, and who have been with the employer for three years must also be covered under the plan. The employer must contribute an amount for these employees which is the same percentage of their earnings as that which he contributed for himself. If he contributes an amount equal to 8% of his earnings he must contribute an amount for them equal to 8% of their earnings.

The money contributed under the Keogh Act may be handled in any of five ways. It may:

1. be put into a trust fund.
2. be used to purchase life insurance, endowments, or annuities.
3. be invested in face amount certificates.
4. be put into a special series of U.S. Government bonds.
5. be invested in a Mutual Fund that has a special custodial account for this purpose.

In addition to the tax benefit from the money set aside under a plan, all dividends and/or capital gains earned by its investment over the years are free of current tax liability. Extra voluntary contributions may also be made under certain circumstances although they will not be tax-deductible. However, the dividends and capital gains earned by such contributions will still be free of current tax liability.

The sole proprietor or professional man who has established a Keogh retirement plan may begin using the money accumulated any time after the age of $59\frac{1}{2}$, and must begin to use it by the age of $70\frac{1}{2}$. Taxes are payable on the amounts withdrawn, but since the retired taxpayer is presumably in a lower tax bracket at that time, and because there are alternative methods of withdrawing the money, the tax liability may be considerably reduced.

TAXES

". . . . but in the world nothing is certain but death and taxes."

When Benjamin Franklin wrote those words in 1789, the concept of taxes was completely different from what it is today. Excise and property taxes were common, but taxes on *income* were not effectively brought into being in the United States until 1862, when the Federal government was seeking means to finance the Civil War. In 1872 this tax was abolished and it was not until 1913 and the passage of the 16th amendment to the Constitution that the income tax became an annual affair. Today, personal income taxes are the largest direct taxes paid by most people.

Income Taxes

Income taxes are levied by the Federal government, by many states, and by some counties and cities. As to *earned income*, Federal income taxes are normally much greater than state income taxes in any year, but there are cases in which state income taxes are considerably higher than Federal income taxes on *unearned income*. Because of the wide variations in the tax laws of individual states, no attempt is made here to discuss them. However, there are certain basic concepts of the Federal income tax laws with which everyone should be familiar.

Personal Federal income taxes are based on a *graduated* or *progressive* rate. Not only does the person with greater taxable income pay a greater tax, but he pays at an increasingly higher *rate* as his income increases. Rates range (on taxable income) from 14 per cent to 70 per cent of income in excess of $200,000.

Not all income is taxable income. There are authorized *exclusions* from income (such as the interest on tax-exempt municipal bonds). There are *deductions* from gross income (such as the $600 personal exemption and the like exemption for each dependent). Also, each taxpayer is allowed to itemize deductible items in arriving at his taxable income.

Neither is all income treated alike. Income in the form of earnings and interest on savings accounts are subject to the same treatment. However, income from *dividends* is not treated the same way. Each taxpayer can exclude $100 of dividends from United States corporations as income in any one year. If he files a joint return with his wife and they jointly hold dividend producing property, he may deduct the first $200 of their joint dividends. This benefit is to partly compensate for the fact that the earnings represented by dividends on shares of stock have already been subjected to a Federal corporate income tax. Until the Revenue Act of 1964, taxpayers were allowed a further "dividend credit and exclusion" of 4 per cent of the dividends from the computed tax. However, the new Act reduced the 4 per cent to 2 per cent for 1964 and abolished the exclusion for 1965 and later.

A tax break is also given to the taxpayer who is over 65 years of age in recognition of his decreased earning power due to his retirement and removal from the working force. He is granted an extra exemption, income exclusions and benefits, and non-taxable social security benefits. These add up to greatly reduced taxes in the retirement years.

Complete personal income tax information, which includes material on capital gains and losses, can be obtained from the annually published *Your Federal Income Tax*, available from the Government Printing Office in Washington, D.C., at 50¢ a copy. It is clearly written and completely authoritative. There are also many other detailed interpretative books.

Capital Gains. It was stated earlier that not all income is treated alike for Federal income tax purposes. The prime example is a *capital gain*. When a person sells something at a profit *in the normal course of his business*, the profit on the sale is generally a part of his *income*. But when an individual sells something at a profit that is not in the normal course of business, the profit is termed a capital gain. If this capital gain results from a sale made within six months of the time the property was acquired, the gain is treated (and taxed) as ordinary income. If the property has been held for more than six months, the gain is subject to a *maximum* tax of 25 per cent of the gain. Actually, the tax is the lesser of 25 per cent or the amount that would result from adding *half* of the gain to ordinary income for the year.

There is one exception to this six-month rule: long-term capital gains distributed by mutual funds generally are reportable as long-term gains by the shareholder regardless of how long he has held his shares. This is in recognition of the fact that the taxpayer probably bought the long-term gain when he bought his shares, even though the gain is actually realized in less than six months.

When a person buys securities of any type (including shares of mutual funds) and sells them at a later date he may have a capital gain to report. Whether it is a *long-term* or *short-term* gain depends upon whether he has held the securities for six months or more. The holding period is from the *day after purchase date* to *actual sale date* . . . not from settlement date to settlement date.

To establish a tax loss in a tax year, a security may be sold up to and including the last business day of the year. To establish a *gain*, the security must be sold so that the proceeds are available by the last business day.

Securities that have been sold to establish a gain may be repurchased immediately without having any effect on the established gain. On the other hand, if a taxpayer purchases substantially identical securities within 30 days before or after the date of a sale to establish a loss, the loss will be disallowed.

Ordinarily, gains or losses from short sales (Volume 1) are considered short-term. There are exceptions, however.

In determining whether a capital gain (or loss) has occurred, the total cost of the original investment (including commissions) is subtracted from the sale price (after deductions of selling charges and Federal transfer taxes). Form 1040, separate Schedule D, of the income tax form is used. This schedule shows how to list cost, sale price, and charges.

Capital Losses. In discussing the tax effect of capital *losses*, it is important to take into account the difference in tax treatment between long-term and short-term capital *gains*. When a loss is taken by an individual, other than in the normal course of business, its tax effect depends upon whether or not there were any capital gains in the same year. If there have been short-term gains, then short-term losses are applied against them to determine the *net* short-term gain or loss. Long-term losses are applied against long-term gains to determine the net long-term position for the year. The net of long-term and short-term are then merged:

(1) If there is a net long-term loss and a net short-term loss, the two are added together to determine loss. Up to $1,000 of this loss may be deducted from ordinary income in that year. Any excess retains its character as a short- or long-term carryover to succeeding years, offsetting gains and up to $1,000 a year of ordinary income, until exhausted. Until 1964, losses

carried over only five years and were always treated as short-term. Under the changed law, pre-1964 losses carry forward indefinitely, but are treated as short-term regardless of original character.

(2) If there is a net short-term loss and a net long-term gain, they are merged to determine the net gain or loss. Any net gain will be long-term; any net loss will be short-term.

(3) If there is a net short-term gain and a net long-term loss, they are merged to determine the net gain or loss. Any net gain will be short-term; any net loss will be long-term.

(4) If there is a net long-term gain and a net short-term gain, they are treated separately. The short-term gain is added directly to income. Half of the long-term gain is added to income, or the alternate method of compuation for the long-term capital gain tax is used.

Corporate Taxes

There are certain basic facts which govern the tax liabilities of corporations.

The *first* $25,000 of net profit of a corporation is now subject to a tax of 22 per cent. This means that a corporation earning $25,000 pays $5,500. All net profits *above* $25,000 are taxed at a 48 per cent rate. From the remaining profit, dividends, which are the earnings of a corporation that are distributed to its stockholders, are subject to an income tax at the top tax bracket of the recipients.

The fact that dividends are actually taxed doubly is of particular significance to officer-stockholders of closely-held corporations. Deferred profit-sharing plans, which delay tax liability, have considerable appeal for such persons.

Dividend income to corporations from investments in the securities of other corporations is treated differently from direct business income. Dividends, if "qualifying," are subject to a deduction of 85 per cent . . . i.e., only 15 per cent of such dividends are added to the corporation's profits for tax purposes.

Property Taxes

There is no Federal tax on property, either real or personal, tangible or intangible. This source of revenue has been left to the individual state and local governments. Some states have a property tax on real property only. Others have an *intangible* property tax, and this includes the value of securities owned. The applicability of such a tax and whether there are certain securities which are exempt from such taxes varies from state to state.

Some local governments, such as New York City and Philadelphia, also levy these taxes.

Estate and Inheritance Taxes

There is confusion in many people's minds about estate and inheritance taxes. The Federal *estate* tax is a tax *on the estate itself*. Subject to certain exclusions and deductions, it is a tax levied on the value of all property owned (including life insurance proceeds) at the time of death of the owner. The estate tax is a *Federal* tax.

Individual states usually levy *inheritance taxes*. These taxes are payable by reason of the *inheritance* of property by one person from another. Life insurance proceeds are usually exempt from *inheritance* taxes, though not excluded from the deceased's estate for *estate* taxes. State inheritance taxes are not deductible from the estate for estate tax purposes, but the Federal government allows a *credit* for State inheritance taxes. Not all states have inheritance taxes and the taxes differ widely in the different states that do. Some states have an estate-type tax, rather than an inheritance-type tax.

In computing Federal estate taxes, the first $60,000 of the estate is excluded—it is free of tax. In the case of a married couple, up to *one-half* of the property owned by the deceased can pass to the survivor tax-free. Therefore, if a wife or husband is the sole legatee of the other, the estate of the first to die can be as much as $120,000 without incurring an estate tax liability.

Awareness of the overall laws that apply to estate and inheritance taxes, including a working knowledge of exclusions, deductions, credits, and computations of probable tax is important.

Even the manner in which securities are registered will affect estate and inheritance taxes. Also, tax laws and personal estate problems change from year to year. For these reasons, it is advisable that most people review their financial picture every few years. Competent tax counsel should always be sought for the best professional advice and services.

Any person who does not have a will is advised to see a lawyer. Many of the problems that arise when a person dies *intestate* (without leaving a valid will) can be costly, time-consuming, and unsatisfactory from many points of view. Intestacy laws vary widely among the different states, but the effect always is to make the distribution of the estate subject to the laws of the state rather than the wishes of the deceased. In many states, there are restrictions as to how a person may leave his property, e.g. he cannot disinherit certain people. The whole subject is a complex, *legal* one that can be avoided if a properly executed will has been drawn up by a lawyer.

Gift Taxes

Many people do not realize that there is a limit to the dollar value of gifts that can be made without incurring liability for Federal gift taxes.

The limit is, however, fairly generous to the donor. Normally he has a *lifetime gift exemption* of $30,000 which may be given away during his lifetime without incurring a tax. He also has an annual exclusion of $3,000 per beneficiary; that is, gifts up to $3,000 can be made each year to each of any number of beneficiaries without tax liability and without effect on his lifetime exemption.

A married couple has the privilege of treating the gifts made by either as having been made one-half by each. Therefore, a husband could make a gift to one child of up to $6,000 in any year without tax liability so long as his wife did not *also* make a gift to the same child in the same year that would bring the total above $6,000. A husband and wife have a combined lifetime exemption of $60,000 that can be used by one of them alone or by both of them in any proportion.

There is a time element with respect to gifts. A gift that takes effect immediately is known as a gift of a "present interest." A gift that is to take effect sometime in the future is a gift of a "future interest." A gift of a present interest is eligible for the annual $3,000 exclusion. A gift of a future interest is not eligible for the annual exclusion and can only be applied against the lifetime exemption.

Special tax forms are used for reporting gifts.

Gifts in Anticipation of Death. There are certain circumstances in which the entire gift situation can be in doubt.

Under the Internal Revenue Code, there is a *presumption* that all transfers of property made within three years prior to death were made in "contemplation of death." That is, the IRS can "presume" that gifts made within three years of death were made to avoid estate taxes. The burden of proof is then on the estate to prove that the dominant motive of the decedent in making the gifts was neither associated with death nor prompted by the thought of death. If the estate is unable to prove this, then the value of those gifts is added to the estate for tax purposes.

When a donor was in good health at the time the gifts were made, was of a cheerful and optimistic nature, had made gifts to the same donees over a period of time, and wished to relieve himself of the burdens of management of the transferred property, a strong argument can be made that the gifts were not made "in contemplation of death."

The three-year clause is important. If a person were actually to believe himself to be dying and were to make gifts deliberately intended to reduce his estate for tax purposes and then lived for *more* than three years after the gifts were made, the gifts would stand as gifts. The gifts would not be included in his estate because there is a conclusive presumption that gifts made more than three years before death have *not* been made in contemplation of death.

Gifts to Minors. Securities cannot be registered in the names of minors (except for U.S. Savings Bonds). However, good financial planning and other considerations often prompt gifts to minors, frequently in the form of stocks or bonds. There are two general ways this can be done. One is through the medium of a trust instrument, which has advantages and disadvantages. The other is under one of two different acts adopted by the legislatures of most of our states. The first of these, the *Model Law*, was developed by the New York Stock Exchange. The second, the *Uniform Gifts to Minors Act*, is an expansion of the Model Law developed by the National Conference of Commissioners on Uniform State Laws.

The principal difference between these two laws has to do with the nature of the property that may be the subject of the gift. The Model Law permits a gift of securities, but not of money. The Uniform Act permits gifts of securities or of money, or both.

As between these Acts and conventional trust investments, the basic difference is that the Acts designate a custodian as manager of the minor's property whereas the trust instrument makes the trustee the owner of the property which he manages for the minor's benefit.

Not only do these laws vary among the states but so do the requirements of transfer agents when the residence of the donor is different from that of the donee.

The exact wording to be used in the registration of securities differs. Typical wording (which varies from state to state) is:

Model Law States: "John Doe, as custodian for Richard Doe, a minor under the laws of the state of Michigan."

Uniform Act States: "John Doe, as custodian for Richard Doe, under the Maryland Uniform Gifts to Minors Act."

REGISTRATION OF SECURITIES

Forms of property ownership vary with the type of property and the state of domicile. *Tenants by the entirety* is a common form of registration of ownership in real estate, yet it is not used in registering securities. While U.S. savings bonds can be registered in the name of one person *or* another, this is not true of other types of securities. A bank account may be held by husband and wife in such a form that either may draw upon the account and the account automatically becomes the property of the survivor should either die. Again, this type of registration is not available with securities generally. The following general rules as to securities registration do not cover the exceptions of a few individual states which have very specific requirements as to husband/wife ownership.

Individuals. For better identification, use at least one given name instead of initials for registering shares. Include Mrs. when applicable.

A married woman should use her given name, not that of her husband, e.g. Mrs. Mary J. Jones, not Mrs. John Q. Jones.

If a married woman has a given name which is not usually the name of a woman, a certification that the name furnished is her given name, not her marriage name, should accompany the registration instructions.

Honorary titles such as "Doctor", "Reverend", etc. may appear in the shareholders' statements and other mailings, but not necessarily in the inscription of any certificates issued to the stockholder. Courtesy and military titles are not ordinarily used in a registration because they are subject to change.

NOTE: It is particularly important when a registration is to be in the name of a single individual that the name be correct and complete. The omission of "Jr.", for example, when there is a living father with the same name will actually result in an incorrect registration . . . the shares would be registered in the father's name rather than in the son's name. There may be a "Stephen" and a "Stephan" in the same family, both having the same middle initial. One given name and an initial are usually enough to identify an individual, but when there is possibility of confusion it is advisable to use both given names in full.

Joint Registrants.

A. Joint Tenants with Right of Survivorship and not as Tenants in Common. (JTWROS).

This registration is applicable when two or more applicants purchase shares together and each desires that the survivor(s) receive total holdings on the death of one of the registrants. It is most commonly used when family members, such as husband and wife, hold securities jointly. The language to be used is as follows:

John Smith and Mrs. Mary Smith as joint tenants with the right of survivorship and not as tenants in common.

Note: This form of registration will usually be used for joint tenants unless otherwise specified.

There are certain definite advantages in this form of registration, but there are also disadvantages which should be understood before shares are registered in this way.

Advantages

1. It is convenient. Property so owned will pass to the survivor without the necessity of a will.

2. Safety from creditors. In some states, jointly owned property is not subject to the claims of creditors of the deceased co-owner. In some of these states, only husband-wife co-ownerships get this preferential treatment.

3. Shares or plans so registered do not have to go through probate and so pass to the co-owner free of executor's fees and some other administrative costs. However, the entire value of the property may be included in the estate of the deceased for Federal estate tax purposes.

4. Jointly held property passes to the co-owner without the publicity that often attends the probate of a will. This lessens the chance of an attack upon the survivor's right to the property by others.

5. There may be a tax savings in certain states where it is advantageous for husband and wife to file separate income tax returns. A husband and wife filing joint or separate Federal income tax returns may each include up to $100 in dividends from jointly held property.

6. Some states impose no state death taxes on jointly held property.

Disadvantages

1. Jointly owned property is subject to joint control. This may prove difficult should a relationship become antagonistic.

2. Possible double estate tax. Jointly held property may be included and taxed in the estate of the husband after his death. If the wife subsequently dies without disposing of the property during her lifetime, it may be taxed again in her estate.

3. Gift taxes may be payable. When a husband, for example, buys shares and has the shares registered jointly with his wife, he is considered to have made a gift of half of the amount to his wife. A gift tax return may be required, whether or not a gift tax is actually payable.

4. Property held jointly may be liable to seizure if a court judgment is entered against either joint owner.

5. Jointly owned property does not eliminate the need for a will. Even though the surviving joint tenant becomes the owner, a will is needed in order to direct the disposition of the property should the surviving joint tenant die . . . this is particularly true should both die at the same time.

There are other possible advantages and disadvantages to this form of joint tenancy, but the above should indicate that the ease of transfer of ownership in the case of death of one tenant should not be the only consideration in registering in this manner.

B. Tenants in Common (T/C)

This registration is applicable when each applicant wants his shares to go to his estate in the event of his death. It is more commonly used outside the family relationships as in the case of business associates. The required registration language is:

John Smith and Robert L. Roe as tenants in common.

Advantages

It provides a convenient form for investment by partners because the interest in this type of tenancy is based on the per cent participation of each partner whereas in the JTWROS type the interests are equally divided among the co-owners. Also with Tenants in Common, the interest of a deceased partner passes to his estate rather than to the surviving partner(s).

Disadvantages

Some of the disadvantages listed under JTWROS also apply to this type of co-ownership. In addition, there is the disadvantage in some cases of having the property tied up in probate over a period of weeks or months with the result that the surviving tenant(s) cannot liquidate shares.

Guardians. Registration should be in the following form:

John Smith as guardian for Mary Smith under Court Order dated

Some transfer agents require a copy of the guardian's court appointment or a copy of the court order authorizing the investment. A court order may also be required to transfer shares out of the guardianship.

Trusts.

Living (inter vivos) Trust:

Requests for registration under a living trust should include the date of execution of the trust and the name of the maker, if not the same as the trustee. The name of the primary beneficiary should be included for better identification of the trust; if there is more than one, ordinarily only one will be shown in the registration, followed by the abbreviation *et al.*

Registration should be in the form *Robert R. Roe, Trustee, f/b/o Sarah L. Lee u/d/t dated* .... If the beneficiary is a minor, so state.

Testamentary Trust:

Registration should be in the form *Robert R. Roe, Trustee u/w/o Mary L. Jones.* A copy of the certificate of appointment of the trustee dated within 60 days is required by some transfer agents. If a certificate is not obtainable under the laws of your state, a certified copy of the will may be submitted.

Executor or Administrator. The correct form of registration is: *Robert R. Roe, Executor u/w/o Mary L. Jones* or *Robert R. Roe, Administrator of the estate of Mary L. Jones.*

A copy of the certificate of appointment dated within 60 days may be required.

Partnerships. Registration should be in the firm's name. It is desirable to add the words *a partnership* to remove any doubt that the firm name might be that of a corporation.

Corporations. Registration should be in the firm's name. If the word *corporation* or *incorporated* or an abbreviation of either does not form a part of the name, the words *a corporation* should follow the name. Care should be taken to make certain that the correct name of the corporation is furnished. The Application must be signed by an authorized officer. A resolution of the board of directors evidencing his authority may be required.

Associations. Registration for an association that is incorporated should be the same as for any other corporation. For an unincorporated association, registration should be strictly in accordance with its by-laws.

For an incorporated association, a resolution of the board of directors evidencing authority for the signing officer may be required. For unincorporated associations, a copy of the by-laws and evidence of authority for signing may be required.

Pension or Profit Sharing Trusts (under Section 401 of the Internal Revenue Code). If there are individual trustees, the form should be:

John A. Doe, Richard L. Roe and Robert Smith, Trustees of The Albert Corporation Profit-Sharing Trust dated.............

If there is a bank or corporate trustee, registration will probably be in the name of a nominee as designated by the trustee.

Tax-Exempt Organizations (under Section 501 of the Internal Revenue Code). Registration depends upon the type of organization. If a corporation, follow the requirements for a corporation. If an association, follow those requirements.

THE REGISTERED REPRESENTATIVE

An investor who is considering the purchase of securities will be in contact with a *registered representative*—an individual who represents a securities broker/dealer. This representative will have passed a qualifying examination of the National Association of Securities Dealers, Inc. or a national stock exchange, or both, if his firm is registered with both.

The representative is bound by many regulations which expressly state what he can and what he cannot say and do in dealing with the public. His relationship with the public and with his employer will become apparent upon study of the appropriate portions of the text in later chapters of this volume.

It will suffice here to say that as an agent of his employer (his *principal*), he is responsible for adherence to law and ethics. These standards are well defined by the NASD and the New York Stock Exchange, and the Securities Act, the Securities Exchange Act, and the Investment Company Act, all of which are covered in chapters 4 and 5 of Volume 1 and Chapter 4 of this volume.

Unauthorized Practice of Law

In dealing with investors, the registered representative must be extremely careful in his advice to customers, not only as to investment decisions, but also with respect to forms of registration, trust, wills and the like. He is always in danger of being accused of unauthorized practice of law should he say anything which can be construed as "the giving of advice or the rendering of any service requiring the use of any legal skill or knowledge."

Because the registered representative is frequently deeply involved in the areas of financial planning where such legal questions arise he will often advise consultation with an attorney. The so-called "boiler plate" forms contain hidden dangers which may injure the client's wishes or needs.

Regulation of Credit

Loans by Brokers. The Federal Reserve Board has broad powers concerning the regulation of credit. One of its rulings, Regulation T, controls *margin* requirements, or the percentage of the value of *listed* securities which can be used towards a loan by a broker for the purchase of other securities. Unlisted securities, such as mutual funds, cannot be used for margin loans.

A representative who attempts to help an investor borrow on terms better than those offered by his employer for the purchase of listed securities or from a bank or anyone else to raise money to buy unlisted securities, is violating this regulation.

The subject of loan arrangements is discussed under Section 2 of Article III of the NASD Rules of Fair Practice.

Loans by Banks. Under Regulation U of the Federal Reserve Board, banks are allowed somewhat more latitude than brokers in arranging collateral loans on securities. The effect of this regulation is that all loans by banks with securities as collateral are under Federal Reserve requirements.

This regulation refers only to bank loans for the purpose of purchasing additional stock. It is quite possible that the loan policy of a bank will be more liberal than Federal Reserve standards if the borrower is requesting a loan for "other purposes" which have nothing to do with the further purchase of stock.

A NOTE TO THE READER

It has been the intention of this chapter to open up some of the problems of financial planning, even though the involved and complicated problems in this field cannot be discussed in these few pages. Experts in law, insurance, and taxes, who keep abreast of changing developments that could affect financial planning, are available for guidance.

Among the textbook-type aids which are suggested for further study is the *Kalb, Voorhis Financial Planning Workbook.*

REVIEW QUESTIONS

1. What three major factors must be considered in a complete financial program?
2. What elements determine the amount of life insurance an individual should carry?
3. How much is needed in an emergency fund?
4. Why should both inflation and deflation hedges be provided in a financial program?
5. What is a conventional life annuity designed to do?
6. Distinguish among annuity, annuitant, non-refund annuities, guaranteed amount of income, and life annuities.
7. What is meant by "pooling the risk"?
8. What are the advantages and disadvantages of fixed annuities?
9. Distinguish between the traditional annuity and the variable annuity concepts.
10. What are the basic differences between the two types of investment companies?
11. Why do the shares of *closed-end* companies frequently sell at more or less than their true value?
12. What is the outstanding feature of an *open-end* investment company?
13. Which type of fund can issue more than one class of securities?
14. What is a real estate investment trust?
15. What are the advantages and disadvantages of the real estate syndicate?
16. Distinguish between taxation of a real estate investment trust and taxation of corporations dealing in real estate.
17. Explain the Monthly Investment Plan (MIP) of the NYSE.
18. In what general manner are variable annuity plans similar to mutual fund plans?
19. What type of person may benefit by use of the Keogh Act?
20. What tax benefits accrue from use of the Keogh plan?
21. Explain "graduated" or "progressive" rate of income tax.
22. What is the difference between exclusions and deductions?
23. Distinguish between the tax on a long-term capital gain and tax on ordinary income.
24. When are mutual fund long-term capital gains distributions treated differently from other capital gains?
25. What determines the holding period (for short-term or long-term) of gains and losses from the sale of capital assets?
26. How is a combined net short-term loss and a net long-term gain handled?
27. What are the two basic tax rates of corporations?

28. How are dividends taxed to corporations holding the securities of other corporations?
29. What is the difference between estate taxes and inheritance taxes?
30. What are the exemptions and exclusions for Gift Tax?
31. What is the prime function of the registered representative?
32. Discuss the basic responsibilities of the registered representative as an agent of his employer.
33. What are the two rulings of the Federal Reserve Board which restrict loans to investors?
34. Can a margin loan be made using mutual fund shares as collateral?
35. Discuss the requirements which the Federal Reserve imposes upon loans by banks with securities as collateral.

Chapter 2

Mutual Funds

BACKGROUND

The concept of spreading risk by investing in many different enterprises is as old as trade itself. Perhaps the dangers of a single investment in a single enterprise are best illustrated by the Latin American countries whose economies for decades depended absolutely on the success of the banana crop. The more stable economies of countries like our own depend not on the success of one crop or one business, but on the *average* success of thousands of agricultural and manufacturing enterprises. Conservative employment of capital by individuals certainly should not deviate from the principals found true by nations.

In its *Investment Companies . . . A Statistical Summary, 1940-1960*, the National Association of Investment Companies (now the Investment Company Institute) says:

Investment companies are the only financial institutions through which investors of moderate means can share directly in the risk and rewards of equity investment under professional management, conservatively, and with . . . broad diversification and continued supervision.

Development

The first investment company was formed in Belgium over one hundred years ago. From there, the idea spread to Scotland, England, and then to New England in the latter part of the last century. These early investment companies were all closed-end (i.e. issued a fixed number of shares that were not redeemable) and quite restrictive as to potential investors.

These companies were especially popular in Great Britain. British investment companies featured many overseas holdings (American railroad bonds were popular) and frequently paid good dividends although the risks were often high. Like modern investment companies, the early British firms offered professional management and, in many cases, wide diversification.

Modern Investment Companies

Although there were some investment companies formed in the United States prior to World War I, it was not until the roaring '20s that investment companies came into being on a large scale. In 1924, the first "mutual fund" . . . an investment company continuously offering shares to the public and redeeming them on demand . . . was formed and offered shares to the general public. Today that fund is one of the largest in the country and has been joined by about 300 other funds in offering shares that may be bought in large or small amounts outright or through systematic investment plans.

During the latter part of the 1920's, scores of investment companies were formed. Most of them were closed-end. As speculation boomed, they grew rapidly. Assets topped $1 billion before the end of 1926. The 160 investment companies in that year were joined by 140 more in 1927, and in 1929 approximately one new company on an average was started each day. When the market crash came, their assets totaled over $7 billion—on paper. The assets of the closed-end companies were something like 40 times those of the open-end companies.

The closed-end companies had a tragic history of failure in the holocaust that followed. Most of them ended their existence disastrously to the financial loss of their investors. A good many of these companies were commonly known as "investment trusts," a misnomer the public soon realized because they were not really investments and the word trust was something less than definitive. The term "investment trust" fell into disrepute, despite the fact that not a single open-end investment company or trust had failed and that a number of honestly managed closed-end trusts had demonstrated good management.

Because of the public mistrust of the older term, the term "mutual fund," referring to a common fund for mutual benefit and risk, came into usage. Even during the depths of the depression some funds were organized. From 1929 to 1939 the number grew from 19 to 64, and an increasing number of brokers became interested in the funds as a means of investment.

Despite the regulations imposed under the Federal Securities Act of 1933 and the Securities Exchange Act of 1934, the Securities and Exchange Commission felt that there was not enough authority granted it under those acts to permit effective supervision of the manner in which mutual funds were organized and their shares marketed. State laws (Blue Sky Laws) varied so widely as to offer no standards, and overall standards were needed for effective regulation.

After exhaustive study and recommendations to the Congress, the Investment Company Act of 1940 was passed. Both mutual funds and closed-end investment companies must register under this act in addition to their registration under the '33 Act. The '40 Act states that an investment company is one which is primarily engaged in the investing, reinvesting, or securities trading business.

The Act was intended to correct the abuses of the 1929-type investment company. It required companies to give their investors complete information concerning company activities and to submit major changes in business policy to their shareholders for approval. Management contracts were to be approved by shareholders or a majority of non-affiliated independent directors yearly. "Insider" transactions were forbidden. Conviction on a charge of security fraud barred an individual from being on the board or serving as an officer of an investment company. Less than half of the directors of investment companies could be brokers, underwriters, or investment bankers. (This last requirement did not apply to "no-load" funds.) A direct blow at the houses of cards often erected in the 1920's was the prohibition of pyramiding of investment companies and of cross-ownership of securities.

The Act proved to be a great impetus to the mutual fund industry. When it was passed, the total net assets of all mutual funds were less than $450 million and were still surpassed by the assets of closed-end companies. Before the end of World War II, open-end assets more than doubled and, by 1960, the then more than 200 mutual funds boasted assets which exceeded $17 billion. The industry continued to grow rapidly with total net assets approaching $40 billion by year-end 1966.

Shareholder accounts also show this phenomenal growth. From 762,200 in 1940, they grew to more than six million by 1966. Because many shareholders hold more than one fund, it is estimated that there are approximately 3.1 million owners of funds.

Several factors contributed to the spectacular growth in assets. An increasing proportion of the population has shared in the prosperity of the last 25 years. Also, the period was one of generally rising security prices which added measurably to the net asset values of most portfolios. Most important, however, was the aggressive marketing of fund shares through accumulation plans which made it easy for the small investor to buy into a fund.

Another reason for the growth of total fund assets has been the fact that many investors reinvest dividend and capital gain distributions in fund shares, rather than being paid in cash.

Finally, the overall liquidation rate has always been less than the rate of new sales. The liquidation rate has been increasing in recent years, but this can be attributed in large part to full or partial liquidations through withdrawal plans and by other liquidations by investors who reached the end of their originally planned accumulation period.

OBJECTIVES AND CLASSIFICATION

Fund Objectives

In most businesses, the measure of management's success is the amount of profit the business enjoys year after year. In a mutual fund, however, the measure of management's success is the degree to which it achieves the stated objectives of the fund as outlined in its registration statement and prospectus.

The measure of success of a fund's management is *not* how well the fund performed in comparison with other funds. A fund should be rated solely in accordance with the degree to which it is achieving its stated objectives. Objectives may vary widely as shown in these few examples:

> *"Relative stability of capital values and income consistent with possible long-term growth of income and capital values."*

> *"Current income consistent with possible growth of capital."*

> *"Income yield as high as is consistent with reasonable risk; capital growth a secondary consideration."*

> *"Long-term capital growth."*

> *"Long-term capital growth consistent with reasonable income return and profits without undue risk."*

> *"Conservative long-term growth of income and capital."*

Even a cursory reading of these objectives quoted from the prospectuses of six funds, shows that the performance of any two such funds cannot possibly be compared. The management of each of the funds is operating under a different set of investment rules. Their actions under a given set of investment circumstances will vary widely, and the portfolios of the funds may be radically different.

Classification by Objective

Different writers classify the mutual funds in different ways when attempting to "group" them. That such classification is difficult is indicated by the many ways in which they are made. One reason for this difficulty is that many funds have both primary and secondary objectives, and very often the secondary objective qualifies the first to a high degree (*long-term growth* . . . and *income*). So rather than group the funds by an arbitrary classification which in many cases can be misleading, we will list the three primary objectives from which *any* investor will seek at least one. These are: stability of capital or conservation of principal, income, and growth.

Stability of capital or conservation of principal. Funds with such a primary objective are usually either "balanced" funds or "bond" funds. Obviously, the investment approach used by the fund management places primary emphasis on those portfolio investments that are least likely to be affected by changing economic conditions over both the short- and long-term. The investment policy will be modified by whatever secondary objective or objectives the fund might have. For example, with this primary objective, one fund might have long-term growth of income as a secondary objective, while another might have reasonable current income as its secondary. Thus, the actual investments made by the two funds would be apt to be somewhat different from each other.

Income. There are a number of different "income" funds, but their investment policies differ quite widely. More than with the other primary objectives, the secondary objectives here have a very marked effect. Where two funds may each be seeking "highest possible current income" one might have the added phrase "consistent with stability of capital" and the other might say "consistent with reasonable risk." Of course, "reasonable" is a term that may mean different things to different people, but usually there is a further definition of what a fund's management considers "reasonable" and examination of the portfolios of the two "income" funds being discussed here would reveal two different groups of securities. One would probably be well-known conservative companies, stable in their industries, and with a better-than-average dividend record. The other might well contain the securities of little-known companies that were paying exceptionally high current dividends, and could include a number of heavily discounted bonds.

Growth. This particular objective has several modifying terms used with it, so no general category of "growth" funds as such can really be made. For example, "long-term growth of capital" is a frequently used term, but we also find many "growth" funds which state their primary objective as "long-term growth of capital and of income." Either one of these may be considerably modified by the stated secondary objective.

Within the "growth" funds there can be wide management differences. They should be further classified as to the aggressiveness of the management. The more than usual risk involved in a fund which specializes in industries with immediate future prospects should be compared with the more conservative outlook of a fund that seeks the type of long-term growth that is basic to the American economy. Within the growth funds are many which are "specialized" as to particular industries like electronics or chemicals or to areas of the country like Florida or the Southwest.

Classification by Portfolio

Somewhat easier than classification by objective is classification by the types of securities held in a fund's portfolio. Here, we have five clearly-defined types of funds:

1. **The Bond Fund.** This is a fund that invests *only* in bonds. Usually, but not always, a bond fund is seeking good income and stability of capital

. . . either being the primary objective, with the other as the secondary. A fund that buys only discounted bonds is still a bond fund, but its objectives may well be high current yield coupled with long-term growth rather than with stability of capital.

2. **The Bond and Preferred Stock Fund.** As indicated, this type of fund is permitted to invest only in senior securities. It may have flexibility as to the percentage of bonds and of preferred stocks held at any particular time, but it is not permitted to invest in common stocks.

3. **The Balanced Fund.** This term is used to describe a fund that at all times keeps some of its money invested in common stocks and the rest of it in cash and senior securities. Usually, the prospectus states the percentage of net assets that *must* be kept in senior securities, though there is not usually a minimum as to the percentage kept in common stocks. Management uses its discretion concerning the portion which is invested in each type of security in order to keep within the limits contained in the fund charter. The percentage will generally vary from time to time as economic conditions change and fund management attempts to meet the fund's objectives under the changing conditions.

4. **The Common Stock Fund.** This type fund is required by its policy to invest *only* in common stocks. However, management may be permitted to hold a certain percentage of its net assets in cash or in short-term governments. There are more funds in this category than in any of the others and there is more variance in the objectives of the common stock funds than in those of the other portfolio classifications.

5. **The Industry Fund.** An industry fund is one which invests the major portion of its assets in the securities of a single industry or group of industries. Thus, though it has its investments diversified, they are spread over one industrial segment of the economy, rather than diversified among several industries. Frequently, the industry funds are found to be more aggressive in their investment approaches than the more general funds.

There is a small, but significant, group of funds which do not fit into any of the five categories. These are funds which invest in highly specialized fields. There are some mutual funds which have been formed solely for the purpose of investing in foreign securities. There are still others which seek out special situations, usually with the objective of increase of capital.

Classification by Management Type

Within the funds themselves, differences in individual charters and by-laws have resulted in two broad classifications of "management companies."

Restricted Management Type. Any diversified fund (as defined legally) can be said to have restrictions on management—even if these restrictions only limit the percentage of voting securities of any one issuer that may be held by the Fund. However, the term is usually used to mean that management is "restricted" by its charter or by-laws as to the type of investments that may be made. The management of a bond fund is restricted because it may not make investments in any other types of securities. The management of a balanced fund is restricted because it must always keep at least a certain percentage of its assets invested in senior securities.

Fully Managed Type. Some funds cannot be classified in accord with their portfolio because they may sometimes be wholly invested in common stocks, sometimes in both senior and junior securities, and at still other times wholly in senior securities. When management is given the right to invest assets in any proportion in the different types of securities, depending upon the sole discretion of management to choose the proportions, the fund is known as a "fully managed" one. Some fully-managed funds have never invested in other than common stocks and are generally classified as "stock funds."

SOME BASIC FACTS

The Purchase of Shares

Basically, the purchase of mutual fund shares differs from the purchase of other types of investment. What is really being purchased is an undivided part interest in a diversified portfolio of securities under professional management.

The investor can purchase shares in any one of several ways.

(1) As an *outright purchase* with dividends to be received in cash. Capital gains distributions, when occurring, may be taken in shares or in cash at the investor's option. However, since capital gains taken in cash are in effect a return of capital, it is usually advantageous for the shareholder to take these distributions in additional shares.

(2) Through *accumulation plans* that provide for regular monthly or quarterly investments. Customarily, all distributions—both dividends and capital gains—are reinvested. There are two general types of these plans which are generally termed *voluntary* and *contractual*. These two plans are further discussed in later sections of the text.

(3) Through a *dividend reinvestment plan*. This is merely an outright purchase of shares accompanied by the investor's authorization to the fund to reinvest all distributions in additional fund shares. Such plans usually permit additional investments by the investor from time to time.

(4) As a *withdrawal plan*, which permits the orderly liquidation of shares on a monthly or quarterly basis. Chapter 8 discusses these plans in detail.

Income Dividends and Capital Gains

Mutual funds commonly distribute substantially all the dividends and interest they receive from their investments after they deduct operating charges and expenses. If the funds did not distribute at least 90 per cent of their net income they would not qualify as "regulated investment companies" under the Internal Revenue Code and would be liable for Federal taxes on earnings and capital gains.

Dividend yields vary widely from fund to fund. The income funds may pay dividends that are three or four times as high as those commonly paid by growth funds. But no matter what type of fund is paying the dividends, the dividends will vary as does the income from securities in the portfolio.

A fund which sells a security at a net profit has a capital gain— a long-term gain if held for over six months and a short-term gain if held for less. As with dividends, the company is liable for taxes on the gain it holds unless it releases "substantially" all of it to its shareholders, who are then liable for the appropriate long-term or short-term taxes. For certain exceptions as to tax treatment of mutual fund distributions, see the section in this chapter on "Mutual Funds and Taxes." Dividends come under the dividend tax clause of the Internal Revenue Act as discussed in the previous chapter.

The great majority of share owners reinvest their distributions. Capital gains, which in effect are a return of capital the shareholder already owns, are issued as additional shares at net asset value. Income dividends are reinvested either at the net asset value or at the offering price, as stated in the fund's prospectus.

Sales Charge

Sales charges are usually between 7½ and 8½ per cent of the offering price of the fund. There are some funds with no sales charge and others with a sales charge of 3 per cent or less.

As illustrated on page 1-41, fund prices are quoted in two ways. First is the 'bid' price, which is the net asset value per share (the market value of all the securities in the fund's portfolio and its cash on hand divided by the number of outstanding shares). Second is the 'ask' price, which is the net asset value per share plus the sales charge. These figures are quoted daily in most newspapers.

Purchasers of a substantial amount of a mutual fund may pay lower commissions. A typical 8½ per cent sales charge is reduced to 7½ per cent for a $10,000 purchase in some funds. For a $25,000 purchase, it may be reduced to 6 per cent. The commission might be one per cent on a $1,000,000 purchase.

Such reduced charges are often available to investors who sign a *letter of intent,* which states that their aggregate purchases within 13 months will total a certain sum. Some funds also are purchased with *rights of accumulation.* Purchasers of these funds are entitled to the reduced sales charges on new purchases when the cost or total worth of their shares still held exceeds the minimum needed for reduced sales charges in each bracket.

Fund owners can usually redeem their shares without charges, although some funds state in their prospectuses that they may levy a liquidation charge. In practice however, only some of the "no-load" funds make such a charge.

Is There a Typical Investor?

No—because people of all ages and occupations and incomes invest in mutual funds for many reasons. The "average" investor depicted in surveys is only one of the many who do invest.

However, the surveys do show that a majority of fundholders have incomes under $10,000 per year. Mutual fund buyers tend to be in the professional and business groups, although retired persons (and the nearly retired) hold substantial amounts. People under 40 years are the most likely to begin an accumulation plan.

While it cannot be said that mutual fund shares have generally been selected by fiduciaries, many institutions as well as individuals invest in funds. It is estimated that institutions hold as much as 10 per cent of the value of all mutual funds. Fiduciaries—banks and financial institutions who administer or are guardians and trustees of money, foundations such as fraternal associations, and business organizations who often use mutual funds for employee retirement plans and profit sharing are among fund holders.

MUTUAL FUNDS AND TAXES

"Regulated Investment Companies"

Mutual funds are treated differently from other corporations when they qualify as "regulated investment companies" by disbursing at least 90 per cent of their net investment income. Then they are treated as "conduits" or pipelines through which the dividends from corporations are conducted to the fund shareholders. A *third* tax on dividend earnings is not involved. However, if a fund elects to retain its earnings, it will be taxed in the same manner as any other corporation. To qualify as a "regulated investment company" under Subchapter M of the Internal Revenue Act, an investment company:

(1) Must be a domestic corporation or entity taxable as a corporation.

(2) Must not be a personal holding company.

(3) Must be registered at all times during the taxable year under the '40 Act, either as a management company or unit investment trust.

(4) At least 90 percent of its income (gross) during the taxable year must be from interest, dividends and gains from securities. But not more than 30 per cent of its gross income may be from the sale of securities held for less than three months.

(5) It must distribute as taxable dividends (taxable to the shareholder, that is) at least 90 per cent of its net income, exclusive of capital gains, for the taxable year.

(6) It must meet certain quarterly requirements as to the manner in which its investments are divided and the maximum amount that can be invested in any one company.

Note that the term "regulated" as used by the Internal Revenue Service has nothing to do with any regulation of the investment company by the SEC or any other branch of the Government.

The Shareholder's Tax Liability

Accompanying any chart or table that shows performance of a mutual fund is a statement similar to this:

No adjustments have been made for any income taxes payable by investors on capital gains distributions and dividends reinvested.

Depending upon the individual investor, such taxes payable could be very substantial—or they could be inconsequential.

Reinvestment of dividends and capital gains accepted in shares must be reported year by year by the taxpayer on his income tax form. The total amount of the reinvested dividends is *added* to the original cost. This sum is then subtracted from the liquidating value of the total accumulated shares to determine the capital gain (or loss) at liquidation. From this amount, the value of securities profits taken in shares *at the time of distribution* is subtracted as "previously reported." The net result is the capital gain (or loss) at liquidation. The same result for Internal Revenue purposes would be achieved by adding original cost to the value of *all* distributions taken in shares and subtracting the sum from the liquidating value. However, this would not accord with SEC requirements in that the SEC regards the distribution of securities profits as "return of capital" and not as a part of the cost of the investment.

It is important that each fund shareholder understand that the Internal Revenue Service applies the test of "constructive receipt" in determining when income is received. A shareholder who has his dividends reinvested has "constructively received" the dividends in the year in which they were reinvested for him. It is as though he had received a check and endorsed it back to the custodian.

REVIEW QUESTIONS

1. In general terms, how is spreading risk accomplished?
2. What two broad classifications of investment companies are made under the 1940 Act?
3. Describe what is meant by the term "mutual fund."
4. Under what Federal laws are mutual funds regulated?
5. How does the Act of '40 define an investment company?
6. What are the two important contributing factors to the growth of mutual funds?
7. What factors affect the liquidation rate of mutual fund shares?
8. What is the measure of management's success in a mutual fund?
9. Explain clearly how mutual fund objectives vary.
10. Explain the relationship between primary and secondary objectives.
11. Why do funds with "income" as a primary objective vary widely in their investments?
12. What is meant by the term "reasonable" in an objective?
13. State how funds are classified generally by portfolio.
14. What is meant by a balanced fund?
15. What are the two broad classifications of "Management Companies"?
16. How does the purchase of mutual fund shares differ from the purchase of shares of any other type of investment?
17. What are the four basic methods of purchasing mutual fund shares?
18. How does a mutual fund qualify as a "regulated" investment company?
19. Why does a regulated investment company not pay taxes on dividends received?
20. When may mutual fund sales charges be reduced?
21. What is a letter of intent?
22. What are rights of accumulation?
23. What type of investor is most likely to invest in mutual funds?
24. A fund owner liquidates his shares. How does he determine his profit (or loss) for income tax purposes?
25. What is the test of "constructive receipt"?

Chapter 3

Organization of Mutual Funds

STRUCTURE

Fund Personnel

Most mutual funds are corporations which issue shares of stock that are all of one class, equal as to rights to receive dividends, to vote, and so on. However, some funds are trusts with a board of trustees instead of a board of directors. These funds issue shares of beneficial interest rather than shares of common stock, but for all practical purposes there is no real difference insofar as the investor is concerned. The explanation following deals with the corporate type of mutual fund. Differences or variations follow under "A Fund as a Trust."

Directors. As in any corporation, the directors are charged with the overall policy decisions necessary to carry out the operation of the company in the manner desired by the owners of the company (the shareholders). Annually, or at other periods, the directors are elected by the shareholders.

Shareholders are entitled to vote their shares in person or by signed proxy. In either case, each share owned has one vote. In some cases, the entire board of directors may be elected annually. In others, to give continuity of directorship, a certain percentage of the board may be elected each year. In such cases, the directors each serve for more than a year. For example, if one-third of the directors are elected each year, then the term of office of each is three years so that at least two-thirds of the directors continue in office each year.

The board of directors is always directly responsible to the shareholders for the conduct of the business and can be sued for gross negligence or deliberate acts against the interest of the shareholders. Usually, the board of directors appoints the officers of the corporation who carry out the day to day activities needed to implement the policy decisions of the board. Sometimes, the officers themselves are elected by the shareholders, but they still operate under the direction of the board of directors.

In any corporation, the board of directors may delegate to the officers or to committees some of their duties. However, such delegation does not ever relieve the directors themselves from their responsibility. Many mutual funds delegate the actual job of investing to a committee, to certain officers, or (more frequently) to an investment management company. Again, this delegation does not relieve the board from seeing to it that the investments made and the methods of investing conform to the stated policies and objectives of the fund. Typical wording in a prospectus is: "Subject to the control of the Board of Directors, the assets of the Fund are managed by . . ."

Officers. All or some of the officers of a corporation may also be directors of the corporation. In many mutual funds, all of the officers also serve as directors. Officers are charged with carrying out the policy directives of the board of directors and are directly responsible to the board. They are also responsible to the shareholders, however, and provision is usually made in a fund's by-laws for the dismissal of an officer by vote of a stated percentage of the outstanding shares. The method of compensation of the officers, usually different from that in manufacturing or other types of businesses, is discussed later in this chapter under "Management."

Clerical. As with any other company, a mutual fund has many detailed tasks to be performed by clerical help. There must be secretarial help to take care of correspondence with shareholders and others, there must be bookkeeping help, and so on. As with the officers, the method of payment for these services is discussed under "Management."

Note: The chart on the opposite page is a guide to understanding the roles of the underwriter, management company, and the mutual fund itself.

Management

Mutual fund management is generally taken to mean investment management. The sole business of a mutual fund is the investing and reinvesting of the shareholders' money. Therefore, management means the supervision of the portfolio of securities held by the fund, decisions as to when to sell certain securities held by the fund, and decisions as to when to buy others.

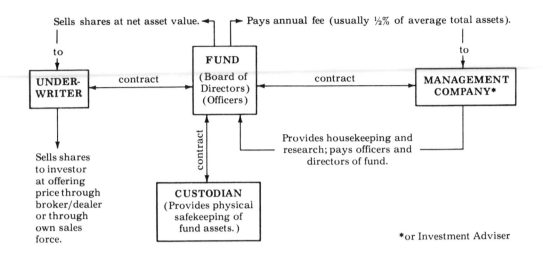

Notes:

(1) Total expenses = management company fee + custodian fee + taxes + accounting and legal fees + printing and mailing of reports.

(2) Offering price − net asset value = sales charge.

(3) Underwriter's fee = sales charge − dealer concession.

This function is generally performed by a *management company,* which is under contract to the fund. In many instances, the management company was originally set up by the same people who started the fund and there is an "interlocking directorate." In other words, some of the directors of the management company are also directors of the fund. (See Chapter 4 for the limitations on the number of "affiliated persons" who can be on a fund's board of directors.) In other cases, the fund enters into a contract with an entirely independent company offering investment advisory or management services. In either case, the contract with the management company must be approved by the shareholders, or by a majority of the board of directors (including a majority of the directors who are independent of the management company), or both. Customarily the contract has an initial two-year term and is then renewed annually. A management contract cannot be assigned by the management company that holds it.

With considerable money to be invested in a broad portfolio of securities that must be supervised on a day-to-day basis, management's job is not an easy one. In addition to its primary job of attempting to achieve the investment objectives of the fund, management actually performs (in many cases) many of the corporate functions of the fund or reimburses the fund for the salaries of fund personnel. Typical prospectus wording is: "In addition to its supervision of the investments of the Fund, the Management Company provides the Fund with offices and office facilities, provides statistical and research information, and employs the necessary clerical help required by the Fund. Also, the Management Company pays the salaries and fees of officers and directors of the Fund who are also officers or directors of the Management Company."

For its services, the management company is usually paid a percentage of the total net assets of the fund. Sometimes this fee is paid monthly, sometimes quarterly, sometimes annually. As a general rule, this fee amounts to one-half of one per cent ($\frac{1}{2}\%$) of the average daily total net assets for the year. If the fund total net assets on a daily average basis for the year were $50 million, the management fee would be $250,000. Some funds have a higher management fee, some a lower. Some have a graduated fee that becomes smaller when the total net assets exceed a certain amount. The amount of the fee and the manner in which it is paid, as well as the expenses to be paid and services performed by the management company, are all spelled out in the prospectus. When the total of the management fee and the expenses actually paid by the fund itself would exceed one per cent of the average daily net assets of the fund for the year, the management contract frequently specifies that the management fee will be reduced so that the total charged to the shareholders will not exceed the one per cent. Thus, it is to the advantage of the management company as well as the shareholders for the management company to hold its and the fund's expense down as much as possible.

Note that the management company is hired to supervise the investments of the fund, but this does not in any way relieve the directors of the fund from their responsibility to make final decisions or to accept responsibility for such decisions.

Underwriter

To market its shares to the public, the fund enters into a contract with an underwriter. Often the underwriter is called the "sponsor" or the "distributor" in the prospectus of the fund. Except in the case of the so-called "no-load" funds, the funds do not sell directly either to the public or to dealers. They sell shares to the underwriter to fill orders placed with the underwiter. In other words, the underwriter does not inventory shares. When the fund sells to the underwriter, it receives the actual net asset value per share for each share issued so that the value of the already outstanding shares will not be affected. In turn, the underwriter sells the shares to the dealers who have placed orders for them at the offering price (net asset value plus sales charge) less the dealer's concession. The buying public pays the full offering price to the dealers selling them.

For its services, the underwriter receives the difference between the sales charge and the dealer concession. When the total sales charge is 8 per cent and the dealer concession is 6 per cent, the underwriter receives 2 per cent of the offering price. Out of this 2 per cent, the underwriter must meet the expenses of preparing and printing the sales literature used by the dealers and dealer representatives and perform all the other services needed to sell shares at the wholesale level.

Frequently, the same company is employed by the fund to act both as investment manager and as principal underwriter. However, there are always two contracts involved and, in theory at least, one could be revoked and the other continued. It is important to note the completely different method of compensating the underwriter and that of compensating the investment manager. The underwriter receives a portion of the *sales charge;* the investment manager is paid a fee from the fund's own cash that is based on the total assets of the fund. The first is a one-time charge that is part of the cost of purchase. The second is an annual fee that usually is deducted from the fund's income before distribution of the fund's dividends to its shareholders.

Custodian

A third contract usually entered into by a fund is one with a *custodian* for the safekeeping of its cash and securities. Chaper 4 outlines the qualifications of a fund custodian. Usually, the custodian is a bank. When told to do so by duly authorized personnel of the fund or of the investment manager, the custodian pays for securities bought for the fund and receives payment for securities sold for the fund. The actual placement of orders to buy or sell may be made by fund personnel or by the custodian, although all of the financial aspects of each transaction are handled by the custodian. The custodian, the disbursing agent, or the transfer agent disburses to the shareholders their dividends and any security profits. The custodian may or may not act as transfer agent. Note that the only real function of the custodian *as* custodian is to safeguard the physical assets of the fund.

For its services, the custodian commonly receives an annual fee that is a percentage of the total net assets of the fund (based on the average daily total net assets) and direct reimbursement for other clerical functions it performs for the fund, such as the mailing of periodic reports, proxy forms, bookkeeping, daily pricing, and the like.

Transfer Agent

Properly speaking, fund shares are not transferred as are the shares of most corporations. However, new shares must be issued and old shares that are being redeemed must be cancelled. This is the function of the transfer agent, whose services are contracted for by the fund. As stated in the preceding paragraph, the custodian may be designated as the transfer agent or the two functions may be handled by two entirely separate institutions.

A Fund as a Trust

When a mutual fund has been originally organized as a trust rather than as a corporation, it is usually controlled by a board of trustees. At one time, the fiduciary responsibilities of trustees were considered to be somewhat more accountable than those of the directors of corporations. However, certain court cases have established that the liabilities of the trustees of a mutual fund are to all intents and purposes no greater than those of the directors of a corporate mutual fund. The trustees are charged with carrying out the stated objectives of the fund and with acting in the best interest of the holders of shares of beneficial interest.

Each trust is an entity in itself and the prospectus must be read to determine just how it is set up. Some, for example, have a corporate-trustee arrangement that assures continued existence in the same manner as a corporation. Most have the automatic termination of the trust some period of years after the death of the last surviving signatory to the original indenture of trust. However, provision is usually made so that the holders of shares of beneficial interest will not be forced to liquidate their shares on dissolution of the trust. In effect, the fund itself may be reorganized at that time as a corporation.

Trusts differ from corporations also in the tenure of office of the trustees versus that of directors. Some trustees hold office for life and new trustees are only elected to fill vacancies. In other trusts, the trustees hold office for stated periods of time and are elected by the shareholders in a manner similar to the election of the directors of a corporate mutual fund.

Investment management, underwriting, and custodian agreements or contracts are entered into by the trustees on behalf of the fund in the same general manner as these contracts are handled by a corporate fund.

EXCHANGE-TYPE FUNDS

As a need arises, an answer is developed to suit that need. Changing investment needs led to new types of investment media many years after the formation of mutual funds. Some of them, such as the variable annuity and the real estate investment trust, have already been discussed.

The exchange-type fund was created in 1960 to relieve a tax problem faced by some investors. These people owned securities which showed considerable appreciation over the course of years. While they realized the advisability of switching from one type of investment to another, they felt "locked-in" by the Federal income tax laws. On a long-term capital gain they might be taxed as much as 25 per cent of the increased value of the security.

In an exchange-type fund, the holder of individual stocks could *exchange* them for shares of the fund without incurring any tax liability at the time of the exchange. Such exchange did not affect his overall possible tax liability, of course, although he might have been exchanging his own portfolio for shares in a fund which had objectives closely related to his own. The investor always received full value (less sales charge) for his securities.

Exchange-type fund shares were not continuously offered as are most mutual funds. They were "open" for investment only when they were organized. However, they redeem their shares on demand in cash or in kind and thus classify as open-end rather than closed-end companies.

Background

Section 351(a) of the Internal Revenue Code reads: "No gain or loss shall be recognized if property is transferred to a corporation by one or more persons solely in exchange for stock or securities in such corporation and immediately after the exchange such person or persons are in control of the corporation. For purposes of this section, stock or securities issued for services shall not be considered as issued in return for property."

Section 368(c) defines "control" as . . . "the ownership of stock possessing at least 80 per cent of the total combined voting power of all classes of stock entitled to vote and at least 80 per cent of the total number of shares of all other classes of stock of the corporation."

Thus, a tax-free transaction resulted when individual stocks were exchanged for shares of a *new*, Exchange-type Fund, because the owners of the property (stock) transferred it to a corporation which was in their control immediately after the exchange. It was a simultaneous exchange in a single transaction in compliance with Section 351(a). After the simultaneous exchange, the fund issued no new shares, but would redeem its shares on demand. The fund was "open" at one end only.

In 1965, the Internal Revenue Service held hearings on a proposed ruling that would exclude exchange funds from the provisions of Section 351(a). The "Christmas Tree" Act of 1965 specifically applied the section to those exchange funds whose exchanges were completed by mid-1966 and excluded them thereafter.

The principal advantages of participating in these funds were the same as in other types of mutual funds.

A possible slight disadvantage in the funds in operation lies in the fact that the capital gains tax in any year on the fund's capital gains (realized) may be greater than that on an equivalent sale of the original stocks by some fund shareholders. This would be true for those shareholders whose tax base is more advantageous than the *average* of the fund shareholders. However, the total realized capital gain by the fund in any one year is likely to be small compared to the taxpayer's total holdings. If so, the total tax effect would probably be small.

Exchange Procedure

Procedures to be followed differed with each fund. There are these things in common, however.

(1) Those securities that would be accepted by the fund in exchange for its shares were generally listed in the prospectus. This list served two purposes. It showed the prospective fund investor the types and quality of stocks the fund intended to administer and it also indicated to him the ready acceptability of certain stocks. Usually, it was suggested that an inquiry be made as to the acceptability of stocks not on the list.

(2) There was a limitation on the percentage of the total portfolio that could be in the securities of any one company. Therefore, although a stock might have been on the "acceptable" list, it was sometimes accepted on a provisional basis as to some or all of the stock offered. For example, if the total amount indicated for exchange by prospective fund shareholders was $100 million and one particular stock was offered that totaled more than

$5 million dollars, the fund might have had to reject all over the $5 million. Stock was usually accepted on a "first come, first served" basis.

(3) Stock for exchange was deposited with a depository bank "in escrow" until the date of exchange. During this waiting period, the stock actually belonged to the original stockholder and he was entitled to all dividends, rights, or other incidents of ownership. Stock powers and other authorizations needed to effect transfer had to be sent with the stock certificates to the depository bank.

(4) If the amount needed to put the fund into being was not achieved, or if the exchange could not be made for any other reason, the owner's stock certificates were returned to him. He paid nothing for an uncompleted exchange.

(5) In some cases, the sales charge for the mutual fund shares was a cash charge on top of the securities offered for exchange. In other cases, the sales charge was deducted from the value of the securities being exchanged in arriving at the number of fund shares he would receive.

(6) The value of the securities offered in exchange for fund shares was as of the date of the exchange, not as of the date they were placed in escrow.

(7) Before the exchange was actually completed, every person who had offered to participate in the exchange received a list of the portfolio that would result from the exchange . . . that is, he received a list of all securities deposited in escrow. If he did not like the list, he was free to withdraw his offer to exchange without any penalty.

(8) After any withdrawals, and upon approval of the remainder of the offerors, the exchange was effected. Each offeror then became the owner of fund shares and no longer had any rights of ownership in the securities exchanged.

(9) Fund shares had to be registered in the same name as the stock certificates offered in exchange. A change in registered owner would have resulted in nullifying the tax-free exchange aspect.

Cost Base

The taxpayer's original cost basis for his securities exchanged carried over to the fund shares he received. An example will best explain this:

Mr. Able bought individual stocks at a cost to him of $20,000;

At the date of exchange, Mr. Able's individual stocks had a market value of $50,000.

Fund shares were issued with a net asset value per share of $100. Mr. Able was issued 500 shares (disregarding sales charge) for his individual securities.

Mr. Able's cost base for his 500 shares was $40 per share plus his per share costs in sales charge and transfer costs. If Mr. Able were to redeem his shares immediately, he would have a long-term capital gain of $60 per share (approximately) or a total of $30,000—the same long-term capital gain he would have had on selling his individual stocks outright. He made the exchange because he did not want to sell the stocks nor intend to liquidate his fund shares.

Taxes

Dividends paid to the fund share holder by an exchange fund are taxable as ordinary income, just as the dividends from the original securities would have been.

When the fund sells holdings from its portfolio *at a price above the cost base of the original holders*, a capital gain is realized. If this is distributed, the fund shareholder treats the distribution in the same way he would any other long-term capital gain. His tax on the distribution is limited to a maximum of 25 per cent of the distribution. In some cases, the fund may realize gains but not distribute them. The fund then pays the 25 per cent tax, which is considered to have been paid by the fund shareholders. Each shareholder would report the total amount of the capital gain as though received and compute his capital gains tax on that total amount. He would then reduce his tax for the year by the 25 per cent of the gain already paid by the fund. The remaining 75 per cent of the capital gain (which he did not actually receive) is then added to the cost base of his fund shares.

No capital gains tax liability is incurred by the holder of individual securities unless he sells them. If he dies with securities worth considerably more than he paid for them, the market value at the date of evaluation of the estate is used in determining the size of his estate (for estate and inheritance tax purposes), but there is no capital gains tax. If the securities are transferred to his heirs, the heirs take the estate evaluation as their cost base. They only incur a capital gains tax liability if they sell the shares at a price higher than that. The same treatment applies to the shares of an exchange fund (or any other fund).

Redemption

Most of the exchange funds reserve the right to redeem "in kind," wholly or partially, instead of in cash. Such an "in kind" redemption would be without regard to the original specific securities deposited—but could be any of the securities in the portfolio. Usually securities deposited by the liquidating shareholder are used in an "in kind" redemption, if practicable. Neither the fund nor the shareholders are liable for Federal capital gains tax at the time of "in kind" redemption inasmuch as no sale has occurred and the gain (or loss) has not been realized.

The exchange funds have reserved this right to redeem "in kind" because large dollar amounts of redemptions at one time could wipe out the cash in the fund and so force the fund to sell portfolio securities to meet the redemptions. This action, in turn, might force the realization of capital gains which would have to be distributed and the remaining shareholders would be currently liable for capital gain taxes which would be "inequitable" because the portfolio action was controlled not by management decision, but by liquidating shareholders. The word "inequitable" is used because the shareholders of the fund have at least one thing in common. They want to defer the current payment of taxes.

REVIEW QUESTIONS

1. Distinguish between mutual funds as corporations and as "trusts."
2. What are the directors of a mutual fund charged with?
3. What are the stockholders' rights with respect to the board of directors?
4. To whom are the directors responsible for the conduct of the business?
5. Can the Board of Directors delegate their authority? If so, does this relieve them of responsibility?
6. What is meant by "management" in a Mutual Fund?
7. What is the importance and meaning of a management contract?
8. Who negotiates and who approves a management contract?
9. Can a management agreement be assigned to anyone else by the management company?
10. How is the management company paid for its services?
11. How does the management contract affect the responsibilities of the directors of the fund?
12. What is the purpose of an underwriter's contract?
13. How is the underwriter compensated for its services?
14. What are the functions of the custodian and of the transfer agent?
15. How are the fees of a custodian determined?
16. Are there significant differences in the liabilities of trustees and directors?
17. What are "holders of beneficial interest"?
18. What is meant by "open at one end only"?
19. How are dividends taxed in an exchange fund?
20. When is a *fund* (rather than the individual shareholders) taxed on capital gains?
21. Explain how an exchange fund might be attractive to an investor faced with a long-term loss.
22. What is the effect on exchange fund shares on the death of the shareholder? Does if differ from that in a regular mutual fund?
23. What is meant by "redemption in kind"?
24. What tax liability occurs in the event of "redemption in kind"?
25. What is the effect of large dollar amounts of redemption at one time in a fund?

Chapter 4

The
Investment
Company
Act of 1940

A CHARTER FOR THE MUTUAL FUND INDUSTRY

The Investment Company Act of 1940 was passed by Congress without one dissenting vote and became effective that year on November 1. Seldom has any industry cooperated as fully for its regulation as did the investment companies, whose representatives conferred with the Securities and Exchange Commission during the investigations and hearings pursuant to passage of the Act. As since regulated, the Act truly gave the mutual fund industry its charter.

The Act was proposed because both the industry and the SEC thought that a new definition of the relationship between management and shareholders was needed, and that overall standards were required to make investment and management practices adhere to certain standards. And, of course, the industry representatives and the SEC wanted to make sure that there was no chance of a return to the abusive practices which ruined so many closed-end companies in 1929.

The basic intent of the Act was "to provide for the registration and regulation of investment companies and investment advisers." Throughout each section of the Act run these two ideas: that the investor be given adequate and full information concerning the company and its investment program, and that the activities of companies be based upon the "public interest." Some highlights are:

(1) Brokers and others in the investment business cannot control a majority of the board of directors of an investment company. Other restrictions on the board makeup are imposed upon the fund management and underwriter. Thus the fund is assured of independent and unbiased viewpoints in its management. ("No-load" funds are excepted from this provision, but at least 40 per cent of a board must be "un-affiliated.")

(2) Stockholders are entitled to elect at least two-thirds of the company directors. A majority vote of the stockholders can also alter the policies of the company. Non-voting stock is prohibited. Investment companies must report at least semi-annually to their shareholders. (Most now do so on a quarterly basis.)

(3) Even before a company sells shares, it must file a complete registration statment with the SEC. The statement must meet the requirements of the Acts of 1933 and 1940.

(4) Any sales literature used by the fund or by dealers and their registered representatives must be filed with and approved (and perhaps changed) by the SEC. The SEC also can regulate selling practices of the mutual funds.

(5) As a check against illegal acts, a protective covering for the assets of the fund is provided through an unaffiliated custodian of the fund's securities and cash and through the bonding of certain fund personnel.

Although the Act also pertains to investment companies which are not mutual funds, this chapter deals primarily with the sections of the Act and the regulations which apply primarily to open-end investment companies.

The 53 sections of the Act are summarized in the remainder of the chapter.

PROVISIONS OF THE ACT

Section 1. Findings ... Policy. A Senate committee report on the necessity for the Act stated, in part:

The Securities Act of 1933 and the Securities Exchange Act of 1934 have been ineffective to correct abuses and deficiencies in investment companies: first, because the record before the Committee is clear that publicity alone ... is insufficient to eliminate the abuses and deficiencies which exist in investment companies and second, because a large number of such companies have never come under the purview of these Acts.

Section 1 of the Act expresses the authority of the Congress to adopt this legislation on the basis that "investment companies are affected with a national public interest." The Section then proceeds to list possible abuses which would adversely affect the national public interest and the interest of investors:

- Lack of information available to investors.
- Organization in the interest of special persons.
- Inequitable or discriminatory provisions.
- Concentration of control.
- Unsound or misleading accounting practices.
- Change of control or character of business without shareholder approval.
- Speculative character of junior securities.
- Inadequate assets or reserves.

The section concludes:

. . . the policy and purposes of this title . . . are to mitigate and, so far as is feasible, to eliminate the conditions enumerated in this section, which adversely affect the national public interest and the interest of investors.

Section 2. Definitions. This section specifically defines those words which appear throughout the Act, such as Advisory Board, Bank, Broker, Dealer, Directors, Exchange, Face-Amount Certificate, Investment Adviser, Periodic Payment Plan Certificate, Principal Underwriter, Prospectus, Redeemable Security, Sales Load, Security and Underwriter. These terms, quite frequently used in discussions about mutual funds, are discussed later in this chapter or in other sections of the text. Governments, Governmental agencies, and instrumentalities are exempted from the Act by this section.

Section 3. Definition of Investment Company. An *investment company* is defined by this section as any issuer "engaged primarily . . . in the business of investing, reinvesting, or trading in securities." The determining factor as to "primarily" is further defined in the statement that any company which holds investment type securities having a value of more than 40 per cent of the company's total assets is an investment company within the meaning of the Act. Issuers of *face-amount certificates* of the installment type are also included in this section as "investment companies."

One of the characteristics of an investment company, as defined, is that it must have more than 100 shareholders (either directly or of beneficial interest). In addition to defining an investment company, this section also deals at length with those companies which do not classify as investment companies.

Section 4. Classification. Investment companies are classified as:

(1) *Face-amount certificate companies.* These are companies issuing "face-amount" certificates on the installment plan. Such certificates are actually issued with a "face" value representing the value at the completion of the installment purchase. The principal and interest are guaranteed and the certificates usually have a "built-in loss" feature since the cash value is less than the amount paid in for as long as 9½ years; the investor takes a loss if the payments are discontinued earlier and the certificate "cashed in." Such certificates are usually backed by real estate or real estate mortgages. They are not equity investments, and they do not classify as mutual funds.

(2) *Unit Investment Trusts.* These are organized under trust indentures, have no board of directors, and issue only redeemable securities in units of specified securities. Voting trusts are not included in this definition.

In practice, there are two general types of unit investment trusts. One is a so-called "fixed trust" which issues shares of beneficial interest in a fixed portfolio. The other is the trust that holds the mutual fund shares purchased by planholders of contractual plans.

(3) *Management Companies.* These are investment companies other than the two defined above.

Section 5. Subclassification. A management company may be:

1. An *open-end* company, which offers for sale or has outstanding any *redeemable* security of which it is the issuer.

2. A *closed-end* company, which is any management company other than an open-end company.

Management companies may be either diversified or non-diversified.

A *diversified company* must have at least 75 per cent of its total assets invested in such a way that not more than 5 per cent of its total assets are invested in the securities of any one issuer and not more than 10 per cent of the outstanding voting securities of any one issuer are owned by the company. Under this requirement, a fund with $10,000,000 in total net assets would have to diversify $7,500,000 so that not more than $500,000 was invested in the securities of any one issuer (other than those of the U.S. Government). The remaining $2,500,000 would not be subject to this restriction. Usually, mutual funds themselves apply the limitation to all of their assets, not just to 75 per cent. (Certain states, under their Blue Sky laws, require that *total* assets be invested so that no more than five per cent is in the securities of any one issuer (other than the U.S. Government.))

A *non-diversified company* is any management company other than a diversified company.

Section 6. Exemptions. This section describes those types of investment companies which are exempt from the Act.

Section 7. Transactions by Unregistered Investment Companies. Unregistered investment companies are prohibited from using the mails and from other forms of interstate commerce.

Section 8. Registration. Companies which register under the Act must file with the Commission prescribed registration statements, statements of fundamental policy, business experience of their officers and directors, and all the information and documents required under the '33 Act.

Section 9. Ineligibility. Certain people are ineligible to act as officer, director, member of an advisory board, investment adviser, or depositor of any registered investment company, or principal underwriter for a registered open-end company, registered unit investment trust, or registered face-amount certificate company.

Any person who within ten years has been convicted of a felony or misdemeanor arising from security sales or from his own actions, or any person who is permanently or temporarily enjoined from the securities business is ineligible. So is a company of which any affiliated person is ineligible for the above reasons.

Section 10. Affiliations of Directors. No more than 60 per cent of the members of a board of directors of a registered investment company shall be investment advisers, officers or employees of such investment company or affiliates.

A majority of the members of a board of directors of a registered investment company shall have no direct connection with its regular broker.

A majority of the board of directors of a registered investment company shall be independent of any connection with its principal underwriter. In practice, there is often a tie between the management company and the principal underwriter or distributor of a mutual fund, which makes this restriction most pertinent. A majority of the board of directors of a registered investment company may not be investment bankers, nor shall they consist of people who are either officers or directors of any one bank. The exception to this general rule is the "no load" (i.e. no sales charge) funds, which do not have underwriters.

The above restrictions apply to members of an advisory board for the registered investment company as well as to the board of directors.

Section 11. Offers of Exchange. No registered open-end company may make an offer to exchange its shares for other shares of the same or any other investment company except at the net asset values of the securities to be exchanged. When such exchanges occur, there is usually an adjustment made to reflect differences in unrealized capital gains in the portfolios of the two companies to equalize potential tax liabilities of the shareholders.

Section 12. Functions and Activities. This section prohibits registered investment companies from purchasing any security on margin or effecting a short sale of any security in contravention of rules, regulations, or Commission orders.

"Contravention" is the key to this section. Since there are no regulations to the contrary, some mutual funds have availed themselves of the right to effect short sales of securities. This principle of investment is prominently stated in their prospectuses, accompanied by a fairly detailed explanation of the manner in which they expect to accomplish these short sales without in any way violating the provisions of Section 18 of this Act.

Section 13. Investment Policy Changes. A registered investment company may not change its subclassification from an open-end company to a closed-end company or from a diversified company to a non-diversified company unless authorized by the vote of a majority of its shares. Because a non-diversified company is not restricted in its portfolio proportions, its management can invest in such a way that the portfolio becomes in fact diversified . . . such action does not require shareholder approval.

A majority vote is also required for a registered investment company to:

- Borrow money.
- Issue senior securities (Section 18 forbids their issuance by an open-end company).
- Underwrite securities of others.
- Purchase or sell real estate.
- Purchase or sell commodities.
- Make loans.

When any of the above are stated policies of the investment company as a part of its charter or by-laws, such a vote is not required, of course.

A majority vote is required for any deviation from the company's investment policy, or any other fundamental policy, as recited in its registration statement. A majority vote is also needed for the company to change its business so that it is no longer an investment company.

Section 14. Size. A registered investment company must have a net worth of at least $100,000 in order to make a public offering.

This section also authorizes the Commission to make such studies and investigations as it deems necessary for "the protection of investors or the public interest, to make studies and investigations of the effects of size on the investment policy of investment companies and on security markets, on concentration by control of wealth and industry, . . . and . . . report . . . its recommendations to the Congress."

Section 15. Investment Advisers and Underwriting Contracts. This section requires a written contract between the registered investment company and its investment adviser. This written contract must state the compensation to be paid the investment adviser and may continue in effect, once the initial two-year period from its date of execution has expired, only so long as such continuance is specifically approved annually by a majority vote of its shares, or by a majority of the board of directors including a majority of the unaffiliated directors. Usually, a fund's charter requires approval by both. Moreover, the investment advisory contract for a mutual fund may *not* be assigned because this section of the Act provides for automatic termination of the contract in the event of its assignment by the investment adviser.

There must also be a written contract between a registered open-end company and its principal underwriter. This contract must also be approved by a majority vote either of the shareholders or of the board of directors (including a majority of the unaffiliated directors) at least annually once the initial two-year period has expired. Here again, this section of the Act provides for automatic termination in the event of an assignment of the contract by the principal underwriter. All changes to the contract must be agreed to by a majority vote of the outstanding shares of the fund.

Section 16. Changes in the Board. This section deals with the requirements and restrictions pertaining to changes in boards of directors of registered investment companies.

Section 17. Transactions of Underwriters. This section outlines transactions of affiliated firms or underwriters which are unlawful. It also describes the lawful compensation to affiliated persons under certain conditions.

The section specifically requires that the securities of every registered management company be held by a custodian which may be either a bank, a member of a national securities exchange, or the registered investment company itself. The securities held by the custodian shall be segregated and subject to verification by an independent public accountant, employees of the Commission, and such other persons as the Commission may designate.

All officers and employees of a registered management investment company who have access to the securities or other assets of the fund must be bonded.

No officer or director of an investment company, investment adviser or principal underwriter may be protected against full liability for his actions by any "escape" provisions in the company's charter or other documents.

Section 18. Capital Structure. This section sets forth the restrictions, provisions, and conditions concerning the sale and issuance of securities by registered management companies.

Open-end companies may not issue senior securities but may borrow from a bank if there is at least 300 per cent collateral asset coverage. Some funds have made provision to take advantage of the leverage thus allowed. This section must be strictly adhered to by funds which have availed themselves of the privilege to sell short.

All shares of stock issued by registered management companies shall be voting stock, and shall have equal voting rights with all other outstanding voting stock.

Section 19. Dividends. A registered investment company may not pay any dividends, or distribution in the nature of a dividend payment, from any source other than current income or accumulated undistributed income, unless the payment is accompanied by an explicit, written statement disclosing the source of payment and the extent of the net depreciation of the company's portfolio.

In other words, a payment made by a mutual fund to its shareholders, which is designated as a dividend, must come from the current net income of the stocks and bonds held in the fund's portfolio. A capital gain distribution made by a mutual fund results from the sale of portfolio securities at prices greater than cost. If there is any departure from this accepted manner of disbursement, there must be an explicit statement disclosing the source of payment.

Section 20. Proxies. The Act specifies the means by which proxies may be solicited from shareholders.

Section 21. Loans. A registered management company may lend money or property unless the stated policies of the registered company specifically prohibit such loans. Most companies' policies do prohibit loans. No loans may be made to a person under common control except under certain specified conditions. The purchase of publicly-distributed bonds and other debt-type securities are not considered as the making of loans within the meaning of this section.

Section 22. Distribution, Redemption. This section contains the regulations and provisions for the redemption of redeemable securities, such as mutual funds. It also provides that the Commission may make additional rules and regulations controlling principal underwriters and dealers in redeemable securities.

One of the regulations is that no registered investment company shall suspend the right of redemption or postpone the date of payment for more than seven days after the tender of such security except for customary week-end and holiday closings during which the New York Stock Exchange is closed or restricted, or for any other period of national emergency or emergency declared by the Commission. There is a statement to this effect in each mutual fund prospectus.

This section contains a very important regulation which states that mutual fund shares may be sold only at the public offering price described in the prospectus. Most of the mutual funds require that each of the broker/dealers who have signed selling agreements with them must act as principals and sell the fund shares at public offering price only. No "special deals" such as reduced sales charges and commission rebates are allowed in the sale of mutual funds. Volume discounts are allowable, however, so long as they are offered without restriction to any individual. An SEC rule defines the requirements which are included in the prospectus of any fund that offers volume discounts.

Any departure from this rule would also be a violation under Section 25 of Article III of the NASD Rules of Fair Practice. This section has been interpreted to mean that commissions on sales made by a representative to himself (directly or indirectly) must be reported as income to himself. They cannot be taken as a discount.

Shares of a registered open-end company must be issued for cash unless they are issued as a dividend or distribution to its current shareholders. However, an exchange for shares of another investment company may be made under Section 11.

Section 23. Distribution; Repurchase. This section deals with the regulations and restrictions pertaining to the distribution and repurchase of securities by closed-end companies.

Section 24. Registration. In order to avoid unnecessary duplication, a registered investment company which has to file a registration statement under the Securities Act of 1933 and the Investment Company Act of 1940 may cross-file copies of the documents required under each Act.

It is a requirement that three complete copies of all advertisements, pamphlets, circulars, form letters, and other sales literature addressed to or intended for distribution to prospective investors must be filed with the Commission by the open-end company or unit investment trust.

The Commission is authorized to prescribe the form for the necessary or appropriate summary of information to be contained in any prospectus relating to a periodic payment plan certificate or face amount certificate registered under the Act of 1933.

An open-end management company or a unit investment trust may make a continuous offering by amending its original registration statement approximately every year. The new registration date appears on the cover of the amended prospectus. A current prospectus must *always* be provided a prospective investor.

Section 25. Reorganization. This section cites the requirements for a reorganization of a registered investment company.

Section 26. Unit Investment Trusts. All unit investment trusts shall have a custodian or one or more trustees with an aggregate capital, surplus, and undivided profit of at least $500,000. This section also provides for the remuneration of the custodian and the segregation provision for the securities as well as other details of the custodial operation, function, and responsibilities. It also provides that a custodian or trustee may not resign unless either the trust has been completely liquidated or a successor custodian or trustee has been designated and accepted.

Steps are also prescribed for the liquidation of a unit investment trust.

Section 27. Periodic Payment Plans. This section provides that periodic payment plans (contractual plans) may impose a maximum sales load of 9 per cent and restricts the manner in which the sales charge may be deducted. This sales charge limitation does not apply to shares bought outright or through "voluntary" plans.

No more than one-half of the first 12 monthly payments, or the equivalent, is to be deducted for the sales load and the amount of these first payments is to be proportionately the same. It is also unlawful for first payment to be less than $20 or subsequent payments to be less than $10.

This section requires that the securities underlying a periodic payment plan (the mutual fund shares) be redeemable and that the proceeds for all payments made in contractual plans shall be deposited with a trustee or custodian.

Section 28. Face-Amount Certificate Companies. This section states the various requirements for face-amount certificate companies.

Section 29. Bankruptcy. This section outlines the various procedures pertaining to the bankruptcy of face-amount certificate companies.

Section 30. Periodic and Other Reports. Every registered investment company must file an annual report, certified by independent public accountants, with the Commission together with such other information and documents as may be required. This annual report is in addition to the standard semiannual reports which must be sent to all stockholders. Copies of all reports must be filed with the Commission.

Section 31. Accounts and Records. All registered investment companies, brokers, dealers, underwriters and investment advisers must maintain and preserve uniform accounts, books, and other documents. These records together with the auditor's certificates relating thereto are prescribed by the rules and regulations of the Commission and are subject to periodic and special examinations by the Commission.

Section 32. Accountants and Auditors. The selection of the accountants and auditors is made at the annual stockholders' meetings. All reports, worksheets, and other documents of the auditors must be kept on file.

Section 33. Civil Action. The requirements for the transmission of documents and records in the settlement of civil actions are set forth. A law suit pending against a mutual fund or its investment adviser will usually be mentioned in the fund prospectus.

Section 34. Destruction and Falsification of Records. It shall be unlawful to willfully destroy or falsify records and reports required by the Commission, to make untrue statements, or to cause material omissions to be made.

Section 35. Representations. No one may represent that a security of a registered investment company has been guaranteed, sponsored, recommended, or approved by the United States or any agency thereof. No person registered under this Act may represent that he or his abilities or qualifications have been approved or passed upon by the United States or any agency thereof.

The only statement which may be made is that a security or a person is registered under this Act or the Securities Act of 1933 or the Securities Exchange Act of 1934—if that is true.

A registered investment company may not use a name or a title which is misleading.

Section 36. Gross Abuse. The Commission is authorized to bring action alleging gross misconduct or gross abuse.

Section 37. Larceny and Embezzlement. Any act of larceny or embezzlement by a registered investment company is a criminal offense.

Sections 38 and 39. Rules; Regulations. These sections give an explanation of the rules, regulations, and general powers of the Commission.

Section 40. Orders. This section describes the procedure for the issuance of the orders of the Commission.

Section 41. Hearings by Commission. Hearings by the Commission may either be public or may be held privately before the Commission, with appropriate reports kept.

Section 42. Enforcement of Title. The Commission may make any investigation which it considers necessary to determine if a violation of the Act has taken place. They may subpoena witnesses and records and may force attendance of the subpoenaed witness through the Courts.

A witness may not refuse to testify before the Commission on the grounds of self-incrimination; however, if the witness claims this privilege, he cannot be prosecuted for his testimony except on the grounds of perjury.

Section 43. Court Review. Any person aggrieved by an order of the Commission may obtain a review of the order in the United States Court of Appeals.

Section 44. Jurisdiction. Violations of this Act are subject to the jurisdiction of the district courts of the United States.

Section 45. Information. All information filed with the Commission pursuant to any provision of this Act is available to the public unless its disclosure is deemed inappropriate by the Commission.

Section 46. Commission Reports. The Commission shall submit a report to Congress annually on its work together with its recommendations.

Section 47. Validity of Contracts. Any contract made in violation of this Act is voided.

Section 48. Liability. This section establishes the liability of controlling persons should they prevent compliance with the Act by persons under their control.

Section 49. Penalties. Any person guilty of willful violation of any provision of this Act is liable to not more than $10,000 fine or two years imprisonment or both. This in addition to the penalties of the '33 Act and the '34 Act.

Section 50. Effect on Existing Law. Explanation of the effect of this Act on existing law.

Section 51. Separability. If any of the provisions or application of the provisions under this Act are held to be invalid, the remainder of the Act is not affected thereby.

Section 52. Short Title. This title may be cited as the "Investment Company Act of 1940."

Section 53. Effective Date: November 1, 1940, for all companies except face-amount certificate companies. Effective date for such companies was January 1, 1941.

REVIEW QUESTIONS

1. What was the stated purpose of the Investment Company Act of 1940?
2. Give five of the most important features of the Act.
3. What were some of the abuses leading to the enactment of the '40 Act?
4. What determines that a company is an "investment company" within the meaning of the Act?
5. Distinguish between open-end and closed-end management companies.
6. What requirements must be met for an investment company to be classified as "diversified"?
7. An investment company has six officers, all of whom are on the Board of Directors. How many non-affiliated directors must also be on the Board?
8. How many of this board can be officers or directors of the principal underwriter?
9. How many could be either investment bankers or officers or directors of any one bank?
10. Would the same rules apply to an advisory board for a fund?
11. May an investment company buy on margin? Sell short?

12. How may an investment company make changes in stated policies?
13. Discuss the SEC studies and investigations that may be made by authority of the '40 Act.
14. What are the requirements pertaining to custodianship of securities of a registered management company?
15. What are the capital structure restrictions on open-end companies as to borrowing and the issuance of senior securities?
16. What requirements must a registered management company meet as to its stock?
17. What are the restrictions as to payment of dividends by such companies?
18. Under what conditions may a mutual fund loan money or property?
19. What are the regulations and provisions for redemption of mutual fund shares?
20. At what price must mutual fund shares be sold?
21. What is the maximum allowable "sales load" on periodic payment plans?
22. What "periodic reports" must be filed with the SEC by a mutual fund?
23. Can a representative state that his abilities or qualifications have been passed upon by the SEC?
24. What court or courts have review jurisdiction of SEC orders?
25. What is the effect of a contract made in violation of the '40 Act?

Chapter 5

The Mutual Fund Prospectus

ITS IMPORTANCE TO THE INVESTOR

No securities of any company which are offered publicly interstate can be marketed unless the company has filed for registration with the Securities and Exchange Commission. This requirement is as binding for mutual funds as it is for any other corporation. Only after the SEC has reviewed a prospectus and given an effective date for the registration can the shares be offered to the public.

A summary of the registration statement, called a *prospectus*, must be given to a potential investor before he can be sold mutual fund shares. The prospectus is the *only* document that actually offers mutual fund shares or plans. No matter what additional literature and information is furnished by the fund, an investor *must* be able to read and study the prospectus. He *must* see the prospectus either at the same time or *before* he receives any additional literature. To read a prospectus is a right to which all persons who are thinking of investing money in a corporation or mutual fund are entitled. The SEC takes great pains to ensure this right.

The importance of this requirement is plainly stated in the Act of 1933 and the Investment Company Act, both of which bluntly declare the necessity of "full and fair disclosure" concerning companies which issue securities for sale to the public. No other sales or informational literature which may be used concerning the security will fulfill this requirement.

The prospectus contains all information which is deemed pertinent in order that the potential investor can assess the company and make his decision to buy or not to buy. It should therefore be written so it can be understood by the average investor. However, even this average investor will often require an explanation of portions which may seem obscure.

It is vital to know *what* material is presented and *how* it is presented. No two prospectuses are exactly the same, but each one contains certain *minimum* information. There is a general pattern that runs through all fund prospectuses and another general pattern that runs through all contractual plan prospectuses. These patterns exist because the SEC has certain standards, not only as to what must be said, but as to where the material should appear in the prospectus.

The remainder of this chapter is a summary of the type of material which appears in a prospectus. Study of the text should be supplemented with the current prospectus of a fund or funds. (This chapter deals only with the prospectus of a fund itself; the contractual plan prospectus and withdrawal plan brochures are discussed in their respective chapters.)

PAGE ONE

Most prospectuses are so laid out that they can be folded for insertion in a standard (#10) envelope. When so folded, the name of the fund, the word PROSPECTUS, and the effective date of the prospectus are usually seen on the front. Some few prospectuses also show on this "cover" the information required to be shown on the first page.

No SEC Approval

The SEC requires two things to be shown either on page one or on the outside cover (see paragraph above). The statement "THESE SECURITIES HAVE NOT BEEN APPROVED OR DISAPPROVED etc." must appear here. (See Section 10 of the 1933 Act, page 1-84.)

Offering Price

A statement must appear here as to how the offering price of the shares offered is determined and must include the maximum per cent of the offering price charged as a sales commission. (Note: In an offering of a new issue other than shares of an open-end investment company, the actual dollar cost per share and underwriting charge to the investor must be shown. This cannot be done with mutual fund shares because of the change in net asset value that occurs from day to day.) Typical wording is:

Fund shares may be purchased from your investment dealer. The offering price of the shares offered by this prospectus is determined twice daily and is the net asset value per share plus a maximum sales charge of 8% of the offering price.

The sales charge indicated in this first page material is always the *highest* sales charge made by the particular fund. That is, it is the sales charge on minimum purchases. Most of the funds, which reduce sales charges for larger purchases, will refer also to the page of the prospectus on which the basis of such reductions is given.

Contents

Either on the front or back cover or on the first or second page is a table of contents listing the major sections in the prospectus.

Objectives and Methods

One of the first general statements to appear describes the *objective* of the fund, whether growth, income, capital gains, preservation of capital, etc. In stating the fund's objective, a statement must also be made to the effect that "there is no assurance that this objective will be met." Also, a statement must be made to point out the "inherent" risks in this type of investment. Basically, these refer to the fluctuating values of the portfolio securities.

Note that the same "hedge" statements must be made in any sales literature (usually referred to as "supplemental literature") when the fund's objectives are discussed. These qualifications are further discussed in Chapter 6, The Statement of Policy.

Usually, the statement as to the fund's objective(s) will be accompanied by some explanation of how the fund's management seeks to attain the objective(s). In some cases, this statement is very brief, such as "seeks to achieve this objective by investing in the securities of well-established companies." In others, there is a fairly detailed outline of the management's investment philosophy.

"No Assurance . . ."

Because economic and market conditions change and because the selection of portfolio securities depends upon the judgment of the fund's investment managers, there is no way to be sure that any given objective can be met. There just isn't any way to know in advance what the dollar value of equity securities may be at any particular time, and there is no way of determining what income any particular portfolio may produce. Even senior securities fluctuate in dollar value and income from them is not absolutely certain.

The only type of security that can be considered 100 per cent certain as to payment of principal and guaranteed payment of a fixed rate of return is an obligation of the U.S. government. The objective of a fund is truly an *objective*, not a guarantee of performance.

There is always an inherent risk because the continuous fluctuation in market prices of all securities will cause the value of the portfolio securities to change from day to day and perhaps to vary widely from time to time. It is quite possible, especially in a declining stock market, that the dollar value of an investment in fund shares will decrease. It is important to realize that even the "blue chips" on the stock exchanges will vary in price by a fairly substantial percentage in any one year. The difference between the yearly "high" and "low" of industrial stocks will frequently be more than 25 per cent. Such a ratio may be true in rising markets, falling markets, and comparatively stable markets.

Should a fund investor be forced to sell his shares when their value is less than his cost, he will take a dollar loss. He accepts the "inherent risk" in the hope that an investment in a professionally-supervised diversified portfolio will result in growth of capital, reasonable income, or some other objective. But he must realize that there is a risk involved.

THE COMPANY AND ITS POLICIES

Type of Company

As discussed in the previous chapter, an investment company may be:

(a) Diversified or non-diversified;

(b) Of the management type or of the non-management type;

(c) Open-end or closed-end.

A general statement as to the type of company usually appears within the first couple of pages of a prospectus. Sometimes, however, this statement appears later under a "General Information" heading.

Typical statements for a mutual fund ("open-end" investment company) are:

> *"The Fund is an open-end, managed, diversified investment company."*

> *"The Fund is an open-end, non-diversified investment company of the management type."*

By law, a "diversified" investment company must have at least 75 per cent of its assets invested in such a way that no more than five per cent is invested in the securities of any one issuer (other than the U.S. government). In practice, most diversified companies extend this diversification to apply to all of their assets.

A "management-type" company may be "fully managed" or it may be quite restricted by charter provisions. The extent to which management may make investment decisions is usually detailed under a heading "Policies and Restrictions."

Reference is commonly made to registration under the '40 Act in connection with the statement as to the type of the fund. Such a reference must be qualified by another statement to the effect that this registration does not involve supervision of investments or investment policies by the SEC or any other Government agency.

Policies and Restrictions

In its registration statement filed with the SEC, a fund is required to state in detail its policies and the restrictions imposed on its management. Whenever these policies or restrictions cannot be changed without approval of a majority vote of the outstanding shares, the registration statement must include the language . . . item by item . . . "This is a fundamental policy . . . that cannot be changed without approval. . . ."

In addition to the policies and restrictions set forth in the fund's charter, by-laws, or other incorporation or trust documents, there are certain restrictions imposed by the Investment Company Act of 1940.

Closely following the stated objective(s) of the fund, the prospectus sets forth the fundamental policies and restrictions included in the registration statement. It is usual for a fund to include certain legal restrictions in this list which were imposed by the '40 Act. This section of the prospectus indicates the degree of flexibility of management and many other important provisions about the actual operation of the fund.

Under the heading "Fund Shares," "General Information," "Capitalization," or other heading, the prospectus has a statement as to the shares themselves. This statement will be somewhat as follows:

Fund shares are all of one class, have equal rights as to dividends, voting power, and asset value. All shares are fully-paid and non-assessable and have no preference nor pre-emptive rights.

Such statements actually repeat the requirements of the '40 Act. Under the Act, a mutual fund cannot issue senior certificates nor more than one class of common stock (or certificates of beneficial interest).

Distributions

Under this heading, or a similar one, the fund sets forth its policy as to distributions of dividends and security profits (or capital gains). Most funds distribute dividends quarterly and capital gains (when realized) annually, but there are many exceptions to this general rule.

A statement frequently found under this heading concerns the fund's policy which qualifies it as a "regulated" investment company under Subchapter M of the Internal Revenue Code. To do this, a fund must distribute "substantially all" (generally considered as 90 per cent or more) of its net income as defined in the Code. Also, the fund may not hold more than 10 per cent of the voting securities of any one company. When the fund so qualifies, its income is taxable to the fund shareholders. Except in some contractual plans, the dividends are taxable whether they are received by check or reinvested in additional fund shares. Similarly, the shareholder must report capital gains distributions as "long-term capital gains" on his Federal income tax return.

It is important to note that state income tax laws vary. In some states, capital gains are declarable as ordinary income. In other states, there may be no tax at all on capital gains.

All funds carefully word the statements on dividends and security profits. Dividends always carry the qualifying phrase "in varying amounts." Security profits are qualified by the phrase "if any."

Offering Price Computation

Under such headings as "How Shares Are Bought and Sold" or "Prices of Shares," there is a great deal of pertinent information.

(1) There may be a statement as to the shares themselves . . . "all of one class, etc." Frequently, the statement as to the characteristics of the shares is made elsewhere in the prospectus. In this chapter, this statement is discussed under "Fund Shares."

(2) There is a statement as to the time when the offering price is determined. This is usually twice a day.

(3) There is a statement on how the offering price is determined. Some funds will give a detailed explanation of how the net asset value per share is determined. Offering price is then stated as the net asset value plus a sales commission. In other cases, the offering price is simply stated as the net asset value plus a sales charge, with a reference to a "Determination of Net Asset Value" section.

(4) There is a table that shows the sales commission as a percentage of the amount of the purchase.

IMPORTANT: The sales charge or sales commission is stated as a percentage of the *offering* price, not as a percentage of the net asset value. A simple computation will show that a sales charge of 8½ per cent of the offering price amounts to approximately 9.3 per cent of the net asset value.

Amount of purchase (at offering price)	$10,000
Sales charge (8½% of offering price)	850
Net asset value of Investment	$ 9,150

$$\text{Sales charge as \% of NAV} = \frac{\$\ 850}{\$9,150} = 9.3\%$$

WARNING: Some registered representatives have yielded to the temptation of greater sales commissions (at the expense of their customers) on what are termed "break-point" sales. The making of such sales is unethical conduct and can result in expulsion from the securities business.

There are two general ways in which "break-point" sales are (wrongfully) made.

First, let us assume that a fund has a sales charge of 8 per cent on purchases below $10,000. From $10,000 to $24,999, the sales charge is 7 per cent. Let us assume that someone has $10,000 to invest over and above a suitable emergency fund. A representative suggests to him that he hold back $500 and invest $9,500. The 8 per cent sales charge applied to this purchase equals $760. But if the whole $10,000 were invested (at the 7 per cent rate), the sales charge would be only $700. It would actually cost the investor $60 more to invest $500 less! There can be no justification for such a recommendation.

Second, two funds with similar stated objectives and similar performance records each have a sales charge that is 6 per cent on purchases in amounts between $25,000 and $49,999. For each fund, the sales charge for amounts of $50,000 and up is 4½ per cent. A registered representative—interested only in his own commission—talks to a man with $50,000 to invest. He tells him that "it would be a good idea to diversify" his fund investments and he recommends a $25,000 investment in each fund. What are the results in terms of net asset value acquired by the investor? Had the entire $50,000 been invested in one fund, the sales charge would have been $50,000 × .045 = $2,250; the investor's net asset value would have been $47,750. But investing $25,000 in each fund would mean a 6 per cent sales charge on each investment. His total sales charges, then, would be $50,000 × .06 = $3,000 and his net asset value would be $47,000. Thus, the "break-point" sale would have cost the investor $750 that he need not have paid.

(5) Following the table of sales charges, there is usually a statement as to what types of sales qualify for the reduced sales charges. Most funds allow a *Letter of Intent* which allows for an adjustment in sales charge when an investor's aggregate investments in a 13-month period would qualify for a reduced charge. Details of the Letter of Intent vary from fund to fund, so the prospectuses must be checked for details.

(6) When one firm is underwriting more than one fund, one may find that purchases of shares of the different funds within the group can be com-

bined when determining the sales charge. In addition, an investor may be able to transfer his assets from one fund to another without incurring a sales charge.

(7) In some cases, an investor's previous purchases of shares (which he must still hold) are taken into account on a cumulative basis to determine the sales charge on any new purchase. This feature is sometimes referred to as the *Right of Accumulation.*

(8) The time period during which the last-computed offering price is effective is stated. Usually one price is effective from 4:30 p.m. one day until 2:00 p.m. the following business day; the second price is effective from 2:00 p.m. to 4:30 p.m. on the same business day.

(9) There is a statement as to the concession to dealers through whom the shares are sold. This statement is generally followed by one that relates to fund portfolio business placed through dealers who sell fund shares. A typical concession for a fund with a maximum 8 per cent sales charge might be 6 per cent. In this case only 2 per cent of the charge is retained by the distributor or underwriter.

(10) If the prospectus is one of a group of funds whose shares are distributed by a single underwriter, there may appear a statement as to transfer from one fund to another. In some cases, there is a sales charge made on the shares of the fund into which the transfer is made. Sometimes, there is a reduced sales charge on such transfers. In other cases, there is a nominal transfer charge, but no sales charge on such transfers.

NOTE: Whether there is a second sales charge or not, it is probable that the Internal Revenue Service would hold that a "sale" of the investment was made at the time of transfer, and the new investment would take a new cost basis. Thus, a transfer might involve Federal and state income tax liability even though the shareholder received no direct proceeds. Of course, if the value of the shares first held was less than their cost, a tax loss might result.

CHANGES IN SHARE VALUE

"Per Share Income and Capital Changes"

Not later than page 5 in the prospectus is a table headed "Per Share Income and Capital Changes (for a share outstanding throughout the year)." The SEC requires that this table give per share information for the last ten years. If the fund is less than ten years old, the information must be shown for the life of the fund.

PER SHARE INCOME AND CAPITAL CHANGES
(For a share outstanding throughout the year)

INCOME AND EXPENSE	1965	1966
Income	$ .40	$ .41
Operating expenses	.08	.07
Net income	.32	.34
Dividends from net income	.30	.35

CAPITAL CHANGES		
Net asset value at beginning of period	$12.16	$14.38
Net realized and unrealized profits (or losses on securities)	3.20	(1.12)
Distribution from realized capital gains	1.00	.60
Net asset value at end of period	14.38	12.65
Ratio of operating expenses to average net assets	.6%	.6%
Ratio of net income to average net assets	2.4%	2.9%
Number of shares outstanding at end of period	3,675,493	4,496,209

Divided into two parts, the first part of the table shows *Income* and *Expense* data. Year by year, the income to the fund is shown on a "per share" basis (usually adjusted to the nearest cent). Directly below the income figure (which is discussed later), is the *operating expense* for the year. The difference between these two is then shown as the "net income per share." Dividends paid per share are listed directly below the net income figure. These last two figures will usually be very close as most funds wish to qualify as "regulated investment companies."

The matter of comparisons is discussed in the chapters on The Statement of Policy. One of the criteria often used in judging the effectiveness of a fund's management is the ratio of *Operating expense* to *Income*. But such a criterion can be completely misleading. A fund seeking long-term growth of capital may have completely reasonable, or even low expense figures, yet show a very high ratio of expense to income because its selection of portfolio securities for growth possibilities may produce comparatively little income. On the other hand, an "income" fund could show a favorable ratio even though its expenses were high. Thus, no comparative expense-to-income ratio figures can really be significant in judging a fund's management efficiency.

The second part of the "Per Share . . ." table deals with capital changes. The net asset value per share is shown for the beginning of each year. Directly below it is shown the *combined* realized and unrealized profits (or losses) for the year. If no distributions were made during the year, the net asset value per share at the end of the year would be equal to the value at the beginning plus (or minus) the profit (or loss) plus the net income. But the asset value of a share is reduced by the amount of any distribution. To give a complete picture, then, the third item under Capital Changes shows the amount of distribution per share from realized gains. The net asset value per share at the end of the year is then arrived at as follows:

> NAV at end = NAV at beginning *plus* net income *minus* dividends paid from net income *plus* (or minus) net realized and unrealized profit (or loss) on securities *minus* distribution from realized capital gains.

In the year 1965, the net asset value of a share at the beginning of the year is shown as $12.16 and at the end as $14.38. Using the formula:

NAV at beginning	$12.16
(plus) Net income during year	.32
	$12.48
(minus) Dividends from net income	.30
	$12.18
(plus) Net realized and unrealized profits	3.20
	$15.38
(minus) Distribution from capital gains	1.00
(equals) NAV at end of year	$14.38

The next item in the table is the ratio of operating expenses to average net assets which is always expressed as a percentage. A simple average of the net asset value at the beginning and end of the year (as shown in the table) which is divided by the operating expenses shown by this average will probably *not* yield the figure shown in the table. That is because the computation is made using the average *daily* net assets for the year. This can be markedly different from the simple average . . . the market could be quite low for ten months of the year and jump up in the last two months, for example. This would give a *daily* average that was much lower than the simple beginning-and-end average.

Following this ratio, the ratio of net income to average net assets is given.

These two ratios must be taken in conjunction with the investment objectives and performance to be meaningful. One fund might have twice the ratio of expense to assets as another, yet the fund with the high expense ratio might show an *increase* in net asset value per share while the other was showing a *decrease* with approximately equal distributions. Because each fund must be judged on an individual basis, the expense ratio is no criterion for judging the effectiveness of the two managements.

The last item in the table—the number of shares outstanding—probably reflects sales activity more than anything else. In addition, a certain percentage of the year-to-year change will include new shares added from reinvested dividends and distributions as well as redeemed shares which are subtracted from the total.

Redemption or Repurchase

Either shortly before or closely following this table is a section that deals with redemption or repurchase of shares by the fund from its shareholders. Redemption is not the same as repurchase. When a fund redeems shares, they are cancelled. Repurchased shares become treasury stock and can be re-issued. However, unlike the treasury stock of other corporations, it must be sold and re-issued at the then effective net asset value.

If the section on "offering price" has not spelled out the method of computation of net asset value, this section on redemption or repurchase does so.

There are certain things to look for in this section:

(1) What the liquidating value is. In most cases it is the actual net asset value per share. In some cases, there is an option on the part of the fund to charge brokerage or other liquidating charges against the net asset value. In other cases, there is a fixed per cent liquidation fee, usually of one per cent. This is more common with funds that sell shares to the public at net asset value than those with a sales charge.

(2) *What* net asset value figure is used. Some funds use the net asset value figure last computed *before* receipt of a properly endorsed certificate. Others use the net asset value computed *after* receipt of the certificate. There are also variations on both methods.

(3) What provisions there are for adjusting for trends on an actively declining market. Otherwise it may be unclear later why shares were liquidated at a price that differed from the net asset values published for that date. Of course, liquidating shares during a sharp decline in the market will hurt the investor who bought his shares for the "long pull." He can only be hurt by panic selling.

(4) Whether the fund has provisions for redemption "in kind." Liquidation may be effected by transfer of portfolio securities to the fund shareholder instead of payment in dollars.

Generally, there is a statement in this section that payment must be made within seven days *except* under certain specified conditions, such as the closing of the New York Stock Exchange by order of the SEC.

Every prospectus contains a cautionary statement that "the amount received on liquidation may be more or less than the amount paid, depending upon the value of the underlying portfolio securities at that time." This is a required statement in the prospectus. It must always be made whenever the redemption or repurchase feature of fund shares is discussed.

GENERAL INFORMATION

Fund Management

Either in a separate section or under a "General Information" heading, the basic terms of the management agreement are stated. Here, as well as in the list of officers and directors, is information about the officers and directors of the management company who are also either officers or directors of the fund. Included in this section are statements covering the extent of ownership of management company stock by officers and directors of the fund. Also, the relationship if any between the management company and the fund's principal underwriter is stated.

In discussing the determination of the management company fee, the prospectus also states just what services the fee provides. The amount of the fee for the last fiscal year is given here as well as in the financial statement under "Statement of Income and Expense."

The SEC permits the fund to include in its discussion of the fund manager factual information covering the manager's experience and the amount of investments under its supervision. Such subjective words as "expert," "highly-skilled," or the like are never used, just as they cannot be used in any other sales literature or presentation. In prospectuses of new funds with other than experienced investment managers, the SEC requires a statement as to the *lack* of experience of the management.

Principal Underwriter

The same type of information is given for the principal underwriter as for the management company. Usually, this information includes the statement that the underwriter is under contract on a year-to-year basis, subject to renewal each year by approval of a majority vote of the outstanding fund shares.

While not so stated in the prospectus, it is the underwriter (never the fund) who pays for all sales literature which registered representatives use in selling fund shares. At first glance, the amount shown as "retained" commissions by the underwriter may seem to be a substantial amount. However, this amount must pay for the sales literature and all of the myriad details of distribution of the fund shares. Because of the legal limitation of the amount of sales charge and the fact that most of this charge is paid to the dealers, the underwriters operate on a very thin margin. (Note: There is no Federal limitation on sales charge on fund shares, though there is a nine per cent limit on contractual plans. However, Blue Sky laws do limit sales charges within the individual states and Federal law requires a uniform public offering price.)

Often underwriters will themselves pay all the operating costs even if these costs exceed the amount of the fee they are entitled to retain under their contract. Such action is not uncommon during the first few years of a new fund or in any fund in which the total asset value is low. The fixed costs of printing sales literature and of distribution do not increase as fast as a fund increases in value. A $100 million fund may find these costs only slightly higher than a $10 million fund.

Officers and Directors

The law requires that the business experience of each officer and director of a fund be given for at least the past five years. This experience and also any affiliation that any officer or director has with the management company or principal underwriter is given in a complete listing of the officers and directors.

General Information

Under this or a similar heading is certain basic information:

(a) When and where the fund was incorporated (or established as a trust).

(b) The fund share holdings of the officers and directors of the fund as a group;

(c) A statement that no person owns more than five per cent of the outstanding shares of the fund, either directly or beneficially (or, if any person does own more, a statement to that effect). This has meaning with respect to personal holding companies. Except for very new funds, a fund in which anyone has as much as a five per cent interest, either directly or indirectly, is very rare.

As indicated earlier in this chapter, certain specific information may be given in one prospectus under the "General Information" section that is given in other prospectuses under different headings.

The Custodian

There may be a paragraph about the fund custodian. This is generally a statement that describes the limited role of the custodian and is followed by wording similar to:

The Custodian is not responsible for supervision of the Fund's investments nor investment policies, nor does it act in an advisory capacity.

SPECIAL FEATURES

In addition to offering shares on a "single purchase" basis, most mutual fund prospectuses offer "reinvestment" plans, systematic "accumulation" plans or a combination of both. Many funds also offer "systematic withdrawal" plans.

These plans vary widely. Each fund prospectus should be checked for individual differences. The plan application forms should be carefully studied for details, such as whether periodic investment payments are made directly to the fund or to a custodian.

In checking a particular prospectus, there are certain specific points to ascertain. These are:

1. Income Plan

The outright purchase of shares from which an investor wishes to receive the income is sometimes referred to as an "Income Plan." Many investors also want to receive payment of capital gains distributions in cash although such distributions are not "income" and may deplete the investment.

The following items should be examined when investigating an income plan:

(a) A minimum number of shares or a minimum investment in dollars may be required. These amounts vary from fund to fund.

(b) The frequency of dividends. Most funds pay dividends quarterly. Others pay semi-annually or annually.

(c) A special form or letter may be required to designate whether distributions are to be in cash or made in the form of shares.

(d) The frequency of capital gains distributions. If they are taken in cash they could vary from none at all during market declines to a substantial amount during market rises. Taking all capital gains in cash could give a false impression of income received and result in a substantial drop in spendable dollars during falling markets when the fund may not be able to realize profits on sales of securities.

(e) The fund must meet the requirements of the investor. It must be suitable for income as shown by its history of dividend payments. (Remember that there are some growth funds which distribute very little income.) Of course, the fact that a fund has in the past paid substantial dividends is no guarantee that the same dividends will be paid in the future.

2. Dividend Reinvestment Plan

Many investors who make an outright purchase of shares have no desire for current income from their investment. Such investors usually prefer that all dividends and security profits be reinvested in additional fund shares.

The prospectus will reveal if:

(a) Such a reinvestment plan is offered. Very often it is not available with an outright purchase but is offered in connection with an accumulation plan only.

(b) Dividends are reinvested at offering price or at net asset value. The fact that some funds levy the sales charge and others do not is really no criterion of the value of the funds. It is the end result of the investment that is important; quite possibly the total growth of a fund with a reinvestment charge will be superior to a fund without the charge.

Security profits are always "reinvested" at net asset value. Because they are considered a "return of capital" from the original investment, and are therefore part of it, there can be no charge.

(c) A minimum investment may be required for reinvestment of dividends. Sometimes the minimum reinvestment amount may be greater than the minimum purchase amount.

3. Accumulation Plans

"Voluntary" or "systematic investing" plans call for regular payments each month or quarter. There are some plans which are less specific about regular payments but which require investment of a certain minimum amount per year. Others are more lenient and do not specify even a minimum amount.

The prospectus will reveal whether:

(a) Accumulation plans, voluntary and/or contractual, are available. Most funds offer one, but not all offer both.

(b) There is a minimum initial investment and, if so, the amount. There are several funds which require substantial minimums.

(c) A definite amount for investment is required, or whether it is a specified minimum amount that may be increased at the investor's option.

(d) The plan requires that investments be in stated amounts: $20, $30, $50, and so on. Thus if a plan calls for monthly investments of $100, it must be ascertained whether a check for $110.45 will be accepted.

(e) The fund regularly sends notices of "investments due" or leaves the initiative up to the investor.

(f) Automatic reinvestment of dividends is or is not required.

(g) The fund allows a grace period before it terminates a plan for lack of payments.

(h) The investor may buy plan completion insurance.

4. Open Account

Generally speaking, an open account is established with an initial purchase to which additional purchases may be added at the investor's option from time to time. It is not an accumulation plan because no periodic definite amounts are required. It usually includes automatic reinvestment of dividends (and security profits distributed as shares). The method of reinvestment can differ from an accumulation plan offered by the same fund prospectus.

The prospectus will reveal:

(a) Whether such a plan is offered.

(b) The minimum amount required as an initial investment.

(c) Whether dividends are reinvested at offering price or at net asset value.

(d) Whether there is a minimum amount the fund will accept for each investment after the initial investment.

5. Withdrawal Plan

There are two general types of withdrawal plans available. In one, the shareholder may elect to have a fixed number of shares liquidated monthly or quarterly. This will provide checks in varying amounts. In the other, more common type, he may choose to have enough full and fractional shares liquidated each month or quarter to give him a fixed number of dollars each time. There are variations of these two general types, but these variations basically classify as one type or the other.

Withdrawal plans are discussed at length in Chapter 8 of this volume.

Illustrations of Assumed Investments

There are charts or tables, or both, in some prospectuses that show results of assumed investments of one type or another. Such charts or tables are not required by the SEC, but are included at the option of the fund. Their purpose is to show how hypothetical investments would have fared over a period of years.

FINANCIAL STATEMENTS

There are three required financial statements in the prospectus. These differ considerably from the financial statements of a manufacturing concern.

Statement of Assets and Liabilities

Statement of Income and Expense
    (for the last fiscal year)

Changes in Net Assets
    (breakdown of changes in net assets for past three years)

Schedule of Investments

A *schedule of investments* (the portfolio) is required as an integral part of the Statement of Assets and Liabilities. Because the business of a mutual fund is the investment of capital, the major assets of the fund are represented by the securities it owns.

In any fund's schedule of investments are:

(1) A description of each security held.

(2) The number of shares (if the security is stock) or the principal (face) amount (if the security is a bond).

(3) The cost to the fund of each security holding.

(4) The market value of each security holding on the date of the financial statement.

(5) The total cost and total market value of all securities held.

Usually, but not always, securities are listed by groups in the following order:

U.S. Government Bonds and Notes

Other Government Bonds (including municipals)

Corporate Bonds

Preferred Stocks

Common Stocks

Within each group, there is frequently a breakdown by industry with the securities listed in alphabetical order.

Somewhere in the Schedule of Investments, there is either an explanation of how securities are valued or there is a clear reference to the place in the prospectus where such an explanation can be found. Also, there is a statement of cost "for Federal income tax purposes."

Non-income producing securities are indicated usually by a symbol next to the names of such securities keyed to an explanatory footnote.

Assets and Liabilities

The balance sheet of a mutual fund is usually extremely simple. In most cases, assets are made up of the securities held, cash, and receivables. All physical facilities, buildings, office equipment, and the like, are customarily provided by the management company. They do not appear on the fund's balance sheet. Liabilities are generally limited to accounts payable and taxes payable.

A typical balance sheet follows. Numbers in parentheses ahead of each item refer to explanations following the balance sheet.

STATEMENT OF ASSETS AND LIABILITIES
(1) October 31, 19...

ASSETS:

(2) Investments at market quotations (per schedule)		$00,000,000
(3) Cash in banks		000,000
(4) Receivables for shares sold		000,000
(5) Dividends and interest receivable		0,000,000
(6) Total Assets		$00,000,000

LIABILITIES:

(7) Accounts payable	$ 00,000	
(8) Payable for shares repurchased	00,000	
(9) Payable for securities purchased	000,000	
(10) Total Liabilities		$ 000,000

(11) NET ASSETS AT MARKET VALUE		$00,000,000
(12) Net asset value and redemption price per share ($00,000,000 ÷ 000,000 shares outstanding)		$ 00.00
(13) *Offering price per share (100/92 × $00.00)		$ 00.00

* For reduced offering price on purchases over $10,000, see page 5.

(1) *Date.* The date given is normally the end of the fund's fiscal year, although it may be the calendar year end as well. In either case, all information given in the Financial Statements is as of this stated date.

(2) *Investments.* This is a direct pick-up from the Schedule of Investments, to which a parenthetical note usually refers. In some cases, a simple total is given. In others, there is a breakdown by types of securities.

(3) *Cash.* The wording of this item differs. It may be shown as "Cash on deposit with custodian," for example. Not all cash is always held by the custodian, however. Where a different bank acts as dividend disbursing agent, some cash will be held by that bank. In any event, this item represents immediately available cash, either in banks or held by the fund.

(4) *Receivable for Shares Sold.* This is for fund shares that have been sold by dealers through the underwriter. These shares are included in "shares outstanding" (item 12), but payment for them has not yet been received by the fund or its custodian.

There may be a listing of "Receivable for Securities sold." This would refer to the sale of *portfolio securities*, for which payment had not yet been received, as distinct from the sale of *fund shares*.

(5) *Dividends and Interest.* As a receivable, this represents dividends on portfolio stocks which have been declared and not yet paid plus interest due on bonds and deposits. In some cases, the term used is "interest accrued." On bonds that sell "with interest," it is necessary to include accrued interest in computing net asset value per share. This must be done to assure that those liquidating fund shares receive full value and that those buying fund shares pay full value.

(6) *Total Assets.* Any other assets, either in the form of receivables or tangibles, will be listed in addition to those above, to arrive at total assets. In some statements of new funds, "organizational expense" may be included as an asset. When it is, a statement is made as to how this is to be written off. Since this is not a true asset, the amount per share involved may have the effect of being an additional "sales charge" to the new investor.

(7) *Accounts Payable.* This is a total of expenses incurred but not yet paid. It may include taxes payable or such taxes may be separately listed. Accounts payable usually includes sales charges due the underwriter and any unpaid fees due the management company.

(8) *Payable for Shares Repurchased.* This item refers to fund shares that have been liquidated, but for which payments have not yet been sent to the liquidating shareholders.

(9) *Payable for Securities Purchased.* This item covers portfolio purchases for which payment has not yet been made.

(10) *Total Liabilities.* This is a total of items (7) through (9) plus any other liabilities that may exist. If a provision for Federal income tax is made, it will be included as a liability. In most cases, a footnote will state that no such provision has been made as the company expects to qualify as a "regulated" investment company under the Internal Revenue Code.

(11) *Net Assets.* This is the difference between total assets and total liabilities. The phrase "at market" indicates that the major asset, the portfolio, is valued at the market value rather than at its original cost. Note that investment companies are unique in this respect. In other types of companies, assets are usually listed at cost or at market "whichever is the lower."

Items (12) and (13) constitute what is known as a "price make-up sheet." In some prospectuses, this is given separately from the balance sheet. When it is given separately, the net assets shown in the balance sheet are usually specified as "*applicable to* 000,000 *shares outstanding, equivalent to* $00.00 *per share.*"

(12) *Net Asset Value.* The net asset value per share is always the net assets of the fund divided by the number of shares outstanding. In the example given, the redemption (or liquidating) value is the net asset value. In instances where the liquidating value differs from the net asset value, the computation is shown here.

(13) *Offering Price.* Part of the price make-up sheet includes the computation of the offering price for a minimum purchase (for which the maximum sales charge is paid by the investor). Since the stated percentage of sales charge is a percentage of the *offering* price, the offering price is equal to 100 times the net asset value divided by 100 minus the sales charge percentage. In the example given, the sales charge has been assumed as 8 per cent. Therefore, the offering price is computed as

$$\frac{100}{(100-8)} \times \text{NAV} = \frac{100}{92} \times \text{NAV}.$$

Reference is usually made to that section of the prospectus that describes offering price.

Income and Expense

The basic difference between an open-end investment company and any other type of business is shown very clearly in its "Income and Expense" statement. In other businesses the difference between income and expense represents profit (or loss). Income in the usual company results from *sales* of the company's services or products and expenses represent the cost of producing those services or products. At the discretion of a corporation's board of directors, either a percentage of a year's profits may be paid to the shareholders as a dividend or all of the profits may be retained in the business.

(1) *Income.* To a mutual fund, income does not result from sales of goods or services. It represents dividends and interest received from its investments.

(2) *Dividends.* These are received from the companies whose stocks are held in the fund portfolio.

(3) *Interest,* which is received from issuers of bonds held by the fund.

(4) *Expense.* The management fee as well as the custodian and registrar fee are paid by the fund. So are the other charges listed for this item.

(5) *Net Income.* The difference between total income and total expense is shown as net income. Normally, the net income is distributed to fund shareholders as dividends from the fund.

STATEMENT OF INCOME AND EXPENSE
For the Year Ended October 31, 19...

(1) INCOME:

    (2) Dividends $000,000

    (3) Interest 00,000

        Total $000,000

    EXPENSE:

    Management fee (see pages x and x)$000,000

    Custodian and registrar fees 0,000

    Audit and legal fees 0,000

    Clerical, printing and postage 00,000

    Franchise and other taxes 0,000

    Miscellaneous 000

(4)   Total ....$ 00,000

(5) NET INCOME $000,000

(6) NET REALIZED GAIN ON
       INVESTMENTS $000,000

(7) DECREASE IN UNREALIZED
       APPRECIATION $000,000

Note: Total expenses were 17.1% of total investment income.

A mutual fund may have "profits" during the year which occur only when securities held are sold for more than the fund paid for them. Such profits are called "security profits" or "realized gains." Note that profits distributed by an ordinary corporation are from *earnings* and are considered *true income*. Security profits of a mutual fund are considered by the Internal Revenue Service as "capital gains." Most of the time, realized gains of a mutual fund are "long-term capital gains" because the fund has held the securities sold for more than six months. When a fund does take "short-term" capital gains, it notifies its shareholders as to what portion of the per-share distribution should be treated as short-term on their income tax returns.

(6) *Net Realized Gain on Investments.* This item is the total investment gain, net of any losses that may have been realized.

The basis of the "realized gain" or "security profit" figure is disclosed. This may be "First In, First Out" (FIFO), "Last In, First Out" (LIFO), "identified certificates," or "average cost." Any consistent method that accords with good accounting practice is acceptable. When other than the "average cost" basis is used, a footnote usually states what the net gain (or less) would have been on the average cost basis.

At any particular date, the total market value of a fund's portfolio may be greater than the total cost or it may be less. When the market value (which is used in determining net asset value) is greater than the cost, there is "unrealized appreciation." When the market value is less than the cost, there is "unrealized depreciation."

(7) *Decrease in Unrealized Appreciation.* From year-end to year-end, there will be a *change* in "unrealized appreciation or depreciation." This change occurs mostly because of market changes, but it is also affected by portfolio purchases and sales during the year. In the sample Income and Expense statement, the term *Decrease* in Unrealized Appreciation indicates that the difference between cost and market was less at the end of the year than it was at the beginning. It also shows that the market value is greater than the cost value. Note that this item, like others on this statement, shows the results of the last year's operations. The actual difference between cost and market values of the portfolio is shown in the "Schedule of Investments."

Changes in Net Assets

The "Statement of Changes in Net Assets" is to be taken one year at a time in order to be able to make year-to-year comparisons (for the last three years) of any particular item.

Since the purpose of the table is to show *changes*, it must first show the conditions at the beginning of the period. Therefore, the first item is "Net Assets at Beginning of Year." Either itemized in the table itself, or as a footnote, is a statement that the "net assets" include the "principal" and the "undistributed net income." The total of these give the total assets (net) of the Fund at the beginning of the year.

"Income" is next shown. The "net income" item is the same as that shown on the "Statement of Income and Expense." This is adjusted by the next two items (see below) before being added to the net assets given above.

The first part of the net income item is worded differently in different prospectuses, but it might be called an "equalization factor." An example will best explain what this factor is.

Assume a fund pays dividends to its holders of record of December 31, March 31, June 30, and September 30.

As of January 2:

Mr. A *owns* 1000 shares of the fund.

Mr. B *buys* 1000 shares of the fund.

As of March 1:

Mr. A *sells* 1000 shares of the fund.

Mr. C *buys* 1000 shares of the fund.

As of March 31:

The fund declares a dividend to holders of record of that date of 30¢ a share.

Both Mr. B (who bought his shares on January 2) and Mr. C (who bought his shares on March 1) will receive $300 in dividends. Yet Mr. B's money was invested for three times as long as Mr. C's. Also, Mr. A's money was at work twice as long as Mr. C's but Mr. A receives no dividend.

In order to be fair to all concerned, the fund adjusts the net asset value from day to day for its projected (or accrued) net income.

The result is that:

(a) When Mr. A *sells* his 1000 shares on March 1, he actually receives approximately 20¢ a share for "undistributed net income" for the months of January and February. This 20¢ is included in the net asset value per share on that date.

(b) When Mr. C *buys* 1000 shares on March 1, he actually pays 20¢ a share for "undistributed net income" to put him on an equal basis with Mr. B, who bought his shares at the beginning of the quarter.

In the financial statement, when more shares are bought than liquidated, there is a dollar figure to be added to net income which represents the income adjustment in the value of shares bought and liquidated. If more shares are liquidated than are sold, a net dollar figure must be subtracted from net income.

To get the total change in undistributed net income (which was an item in net assets), the dividends paid out by the fund are subtracted from the net income as adjusted for the equalization factor.

We next find the change resulting from realized gains. First, the amount of such gains is given and then the amount distributed is given. The difference (if any) is part of the net change that is being developed for the year.

After realized gains, the *change* in *unrealized gains* is given.

For any shares issued by the fund during the year, the amount of cash received is shown. For any shares redeemed by the fund during the year, cash was paid out. This amount is also shown. The *difference* between these two sums is a part of the *change* since the beginning of the year.

The last item shown is the total of net assets at the *end* of the year.

This represents:

Net assets at beginning
(plus) Net income
(plus or minus) Equalization factor
(minus) Dividends paid to Fund Shareholders
(plus) Realized gains
(minus) Distributions of realized gains
(plus or minus) Change in unrealized gains or losses
(plus) * Receipts for Fund Shares sold
(minus) Cost of Fund Shares redeemed

In some, but not all, prospectuses there is an additional heading, "Statement of Sources of Net Assets."

Whether so stated or not, all footnotes relating to the financial statements are considered a part of the statements themselves, and the statements cannot be considered complete without them.

Auditor's Report

The '40 Act requires an annual audit by "independent" accountants. Because the financial statements given in the prospectus are audited statements, an "Auditor's Report" is always included with the financial statements.

Officers

Officers of the fund, and of various affiliates, are frequently listed on the back cover.

Omitted Information

Often a statement similar to the following is found:

This prospectus omits certain information contained in the registration statement filed with the Securities and Exchange Commission. Items of information thus omitted may be obtained from the Securities and Exchange Commission upon payment of the fee prescribed by the regulations.

Generally speaking, technical information, including financial information about affiliates that the SEC does not regard as essential to the "full and fair disclosure" provisions of the '33 Act has been left out. The omitted information is not considered by the SEC as vital or necessary in understanding the financial and operational aspects of the fund.

---

* Adjusted for "equalization factor" shown under "income."

The Self-Employed Retirement Act.

Shares of most funds can now be purchased by self-employed individuals, such as physicians, lawyers, and small businessmen, in conjunction with the Self-Employed Individuals Tax Retirement Act of 1962.

When available, the investor is required to sign an agreement between himself and the custodian. Normally, the purchaser pays a clerical charge for opening and maintaining the account for himself and/or his employees.

Funds offering shares under this Act announce that fact in the prospectus.

REVIEW QUESTIONS

1. When must a mutual fund prospectus be presented to a potential investor?
2. How often are offering prices usually determined?
3. What statement must appear with the statement of a fund's objective?
4. Describe the "inherent risk" in equity investments.
5. What normal fluctuations in market value of common stocks might be expected during a year?
6. What is meant by an "open-end, managed, diversified investment company"?
7. Discuss "policies and restrictions" of a mutual fund.
8. What information is given in a prospectus about distributions?
9. When is an investment company exempt from Federal income tax?
10. Distinguish between sales charge as a percentage of net asset value and as a percentage of offering price.
11. What is a "break-point" sale?
12. What is a "letter of intent"?
13. What is meant by "right of accumulation"? Explain its effect.
14. Discuss transfer from one mutual fund to another. Explain costs and possible tax effects.
15. What significance has the operating expense to income ratio?
16. What is the significance of the operating expenses to average net asset ratio?
17. What possible difference can there be between net asset value and liquidating value?
18. What is redemption "in kind"?
19. What is the length of time allowed for payment on redemption?
20. For what does the underwriter pay?
21. What is the role of the custodian?
22. What is meant by an income plan?
23. What should one look for in a dividend reinvestment plan?
24. What eight things are there to know about an accumulation plan offered in a prospectus?
25. Distinguish between an "accumulation plan" and an "open account."
26. Explain the difference between the two general types of withdrawal plans?
27. What are the three financial statements required in a prospectus?
28. How do these statements compare in general with statements of manufacturing concerns?
29. What are included under assets and liabilities of a fund?

30. Explain each of the following in a financial statement of a fund:
    a. Investments
    b. Cash
    c. Receivable for shares sold
    d. Receivable for securities sold
    e. Dividends and interest receivable
    f. Total assets
    g. Accounts payable
    h. Payable for shares repurchased
    i. Payable for securities
    j. Total liabilities
    k. Net assets
    l. Net asset value
    m. Offering price

31. What is the basic difference between income to an open-end investment company and profit of other types of companies?

32. Who determines the amount of profits distributed by an industrial corporation?

33. How are mutual fund "security profits" treated for tax purposes by the shareholders?

34. What is unrealized appreciation? Unrealized depreciation?

35. Explain how the equalization factor makes it disadvantageous for anyone to buy shares just before a fund goes "ex-dividend."

Chapter 6

The SEC's Statement of Policy

ITS PURPOSE

In the ten years following the passage of the Act of 1940, it became apparent to the Securities and Exchange Commission that its regulations alone were not enough to define three broad areas in the marketing of fund shares.

The SEC, in attempting to set standards of sales practices, was concerned with:

1. What *may* be said to prospective investors.
2. What *may not* be said.
3. What *must* be said.

With the assistance of the National Association of Securities Dealers, Inc., the SEC reviewed samples of sales literature and advertising that had been used up to 1950. As a result of its findings, the SEC issued a Statement of Policy on August 1, 1950 as a guide against violations of the statutory requirements of the Acts of '33 and '40. The Statement of Policy is reviewed constantly, and from time to time is amended to keep abreast of changing conditions.

HOW IT IS USED

At first glance the Statement of Policy may appear as a stern "don't" list. It might seem that mutual funds and all other securities could not be marketed legally in any fashion if the industry were to adhere to the SOP.

The Statement of Policy should be properly viewed as a guide to an honest job of presentation. In point of fact, the SOP is the government's interpretation of its own law, though it specifically states that this interpretation does not cover all possible violations which might occur.

There is one important word which recurs constantly in the Statement of Policy. That word, "literature", is used in a very inclusive sense to mean everything *said* as well as everything which is printed, mimeographed, or written for public consumption. Thus, even an oral statement is "sales literature."

In its introduction to the Statement of Policy, the SEC emphasizes that it cannot predict what twist might be put on words at some time in the fuure. The SEC thus states that all material presented to the public must be in such a form that it will not mislead. Thus, the Statement of Policy

. . . does not attempt to cover all possible abuses, and that literature which complies with this statement may not be used if it is in fact misleading.

Conversely, nothing in this Statement of Policy is intended to prevent the use of factual statements, fairly presented, concerning fundamental investment policies and objectives, investment restrictions or other characteristics of a particular investment company.

Sales Literature Defined

The next statement starts the definition of sales literature:

> *"Sales literature" as used hereafter shall be deemed to include any communication (whether in writing, by radio or by television) used by an issuer, underwriter or dealer to induce the purchase of shares of an investment company.*

Two important ideas are brought out in this sentence: "*any communication*" is amplified in parentheses "*(whether in writing, by radio or by television).*" Although not expressly stated, "*any communication*" includes word-of-mouth communication. When the word "dealer" is used, it is understood to mean dealer-salesmen or registered representatives, just as it means the dealer himself. Because a registered representative represents the dealer, he speaks for the dealer. Therefore, what applies to the dealer also applies to his representative. The representative never represents the fund itself, but he may, under certain circumstances, represent the fund underwriter.

The definition of sales literature continues:

Reports (such as quarterly and annual reports) of *issuers* (that is, issuers of shares . . . mutual funds) *to the extent they are transmitted to shareholders and do not contain an express offer are not deemed to be "sales literature" within the meaning of this definition but shall conform to this Statement of Policy.*

Although semi-annual and annual reports or any other reports to share-holders are not classified as sales literature when they are delivered to shareholders, they are considered as sales literature when they are used in connection with a sales presentation. Such a report is also "sales literature" when used to induce a present shareholder to increase his investment in the fund.

Letters or other information exchanged between issuers or dealers and representatives are usually to be considered "*sales literature.*" Routine business matters, of course, are excepted.

> *Communications between issuers, underwriters and dealers are included in this definition of "sales literature" only if such communications are passed on either orally or in writing or are shown to prospective investors or were designed to be employed in either written or oral form in the sale of securities.*

Most of the material provided to representatives is intended for showing to prospects or to assist in oral presentations of sales material. Such information therefore, must be thought of as "*sales literature.*"

> *For the purpose of interpreting this Statement of Policy, a piece of sales literature shall be deemed material-ly misleading by reason of an implication, as contemplated herein, if such sales literature (1) includes an untrue state-ment of a material fact or (2) omits a material fact neces-sary in order to make a statement made, in the light of the circumstances of its use, not misleading.*

Statement (1) is obvious. It is quite apparent that inclusion of an untrue statement would make any material misleading. But (2) can be confusing to a great many people. Perhaps it is best explained by an example.

A used car salesman makes the following statement. "This is a one owner car that we have serviced since it was new. We *know* this car!" This is a statement that can have more than one meaning. He *hopes* the customer will take it to mean that a gentle, old lady drove it very carefully just a few miles a day and that the car was serviced in the best possible way since the car was new. But what happens to the customer's feeling about the car if he adds: "Of course, the owner smashed it up several times, and we only serviced it when it was brought in for repairs!"

His first statement was a statement of fact. Yet that statement of fact was completely misleading without another statement of fact. In describing shares of any mutual fund *all* the essential facts, even the unpleasant ones, must be presented.

"Materially Misleading . . ."

After the general introductory statements which define its scope, the Statement of Policy becomes more detailed. Each new section is preceded by:

> *It will be considered materially misleading hereafter for sales literature . . .*

The key here is to realize what the SEC means when it says "materially misleading." A violation of this clause is a clear violation of the fraud section of the '33 Act.

> *It shall be unlawful for any person in the sale of any securities by use of transportation or communication in interstate commerce or by use of the mails to employ a device or scheme to defraud, to obtain money or property by means of any untrue statement or omission, to engage in any transaction that would operate as a fraud.*

"What Is Fund X's Rate of Return?"

One of the many questions asked about a fund is, "What rate of return did the fund pay last year?"

The SEC specifically says what the reply can and cannot be:

It will be considered materially misleading hereafter for sales literature—

(a) *To represent or imply a percentage return on an investment in the shares of an investment company unless based upon—*

> (1) *Dividends from net investment income paid during a fiscal year related to the average monthly offering price for such fiscal year, provided that if any year prior to the most recent fiscal year is selected for this purpose, the rate of return for all subsequent fiscal years, similarly calculated, shall also be stated, or*

> (2) *Dividends paid from net investment income during the twelve months ending not earlier than the close of the calendar month immediately preceding the date of publication related to an offering price current at said date of publication;*

in either case the basis of the calculation shall be shown and adjustment made for capital gains distributions and any other factor necessary to make the presentation not misleading. 'Net investment income' as used above shall include net accrued undivided earnings included in the price of capital shares issued and repurchased and shall be as required to be included in the issuer's prospectus. Every such statement of return shall be accompanied by a statement to the effect that such return is based upon dividends paid in the period covered and is not a representation of future results. Either in the same text, or by reference in the same text to an historical table elsewhere in the same piece of literature, there must be shown the per-share asset value at the beginning and end of the period, or the increase or decrease (stated in percentages) in asset value.

This somewhat complicated set of requirements might indicate that it would be difficult to express a rate of return. Because dividends and per share assets vary from year to year, a direct answer to that question could be most confusing. It is not begging the issue if the investor is advised that the concept of investing in the shares of a mutual fund is so completely different from that of putting money into the bank, where you get a stated rate of interest, that any answer given might be misleading.

Percentage returns tell only a small part of the mutual fund story for those who invest for long-range purposes. The investor cannot expect to hear or read an involved explanation unless he is primarily interested in income. Then, of course, the current indicated dividend return is of prime importance.

In this case, the investor should hear an explanation based on the guidelines in paragraph (a) (1) for the last fiscal year. If the fund literature gives the net investment income for any year other than the last, the net investment income must also be given for every fiscal year from that year up to the present.

In its booklet *What you Must Know* . . . the NASD explains how the fiscal year percentage return should be stated.

Dividends from Income for fiscal 19. . .	*$ 0.75*
Average Monthly Offering Price for fiscal 19. . .	*$18.75*
Rate of Return ($.75 divided by $18.75)	*4%*

To answer the question, then, "Based on an average monthly offering price of $18.75 per share and dividends from net investment income of 75¢ per share during fiscal year 19—, the fund paid a return of four per cent."

Not only is this statement involved, it will be probably confusing. And even this statement is not in accord with the Statement of Policy!

Note the last two sentences in section (a) . . . in addition to what has been said above, it would have to add that the statement is not indicative of future results and another statement as to the change in net asset value per share during the fiscal year. Here is what should be said.

"Based on an average monthly offering price of $18.75 per share and dividends from net investment income of 75¢ per share during fiscal 19—, the fund paid a return of four per cent. Of course, this is based on the dividends paid during this particular period of time and cannot be taken as representative of future results. During fiscal 19—, the net asset value per share, adjusted for capital gains distributions, increased $1.50 (or 8 per cent per share)."

The SEC is not being capricious or unrealistic in demanding such statements. These restrictions apply to *percentage* return, *not* to return in terms of dollars and cents. The investor can be effectively shown what an investment in shares of a specific mutual fund would have meant in terms of real income by reference to the historical dollar figures. But percentage return has real meaning only when a guaranteed rate is given on a debt-type security. On an ownership type of security, such as shares of a mutual fund, other factors enter the picture, such as increase or decrease in the value of the investment.

Percentage figures should be avoided whenever possible in connnection with mutual fund shares. People generally relate percentage to savings accounts and government bonds which are manifestly different from mutual fund shares. Just as the word "annuity" has come to mean a "guaranteed, fixed number of dollars per year" in the public mind, so has the term "percentage" evolved into the idea of a return which is definitely expected to be continued, if not guaranteed. Such a concept of debt-free investment differs completely from the concept of mutual funds.

For two good reasons the SEC restricted the manner in which percentage returns can be stated.

(1) Unless presented extremely carefully, the fact that a percentage is used at all may imply that such a return could reasonably be expected to continue.

(2) Although the above is really enough, there are reasons which are based on the accurate and factual computation of investment results. Strictly speaking, the only type of dividend or distribution that can properly be used in a percentage return is one that uses true net income. By definition, an investment company derives its income *only* from its investments. Furthermore, the fund's expenses must be paid from that income. Therefore, the only true income to the shareholder is his share of the net income—or what is left of the fund's investment income after it has paid its expenses. In addition to this factor, the calculation of net income must be based on the investor's cost, which in the case of a mutual fund would be the offering price paid by the investor; it would not be the current net asset value.

Presentation of Distributions

It will be considered materially misleading hereafter for sales literature—

(b)(1) *To combine into any one amount distributions from net investment income and distributions from any other source.*

According to the NASD, this is the most frequently violated section of the Statement of Policy. There are several ways in which this section can be violated. *All of the following statements are violations:*

> "The fund paid $1.93 a share in dividends plus $1.07 a share in security profits during the last year . . . a total of $3.00 per share . . . which is about eight per cent of the average monthly offering price during the year."

> "Dividends were three per cent of offering price and capital gains paid out were four per cent." (Note that this is a violation even though the three per cent and the four per cent were not added together . . . the wording was such that a listener could not help but add them together in his mind.)

> "We paid $1.93 a share in ordinary dividends plus $1.07 a share in special dividends, or $3 a share last year."

> "Combined dividends and capital gains were $3 a share last year."

There is a proper way to make a statement that brings together the dividends from income and the distributions of capital gains. But this proper way is like adding apples and oranges. Four apples plus three oranges equals seven pieces of fruit, *not* seven apples or seven oranges. This kind of addition can be confusing, because it obscures the facts.

No one is banned from talking about the dividends from net investments and distributions from security profits *if* he tells the *whole* story. The problem again is that the whole story becomes confusing to any but a knowledgeable investor. When stated as in the example below, it would seem better if the representative presented the idea of mutual fund shares in a different way.

Here's how it can be done under sections (a) and (b):

"During the last fiscal year, the fund paid 20¢ a share in dividends from net investment income, which is four percent of the average monthly offering price of $5 a share during that fiscal year. At the same time, the net asset value per share rose from $4.24 at the beginning of the period to $4.74 at the end of the period adjusted for a capital gain distribution of 17¢ a share."

But such a confusing statement (however accurate) will serve only to confuse instead of help someone who is not familiar with mutual funds.

Fortunately, there is a valuable aid in the form of the historical record of the fund. This record will have been prepared by the fund underwriter and cleared with the SEC, the NASD, or both. It can be studied by any investor who really wants to know for any particular year, or for all the years the fund has been in business, just how much has been paid to share-holders in dividends and in capital gains.

But under no circumstances should these be added together.

Security profits are to dividends as apples are to oranges because:

Dividends are paid from net investment income. They are the interest and dividends received from the mutual fund from the portfolio companies less the fund's expenses of operation during the year. Because the dividends from portfolio companies vary and the fund's expenses are not always the same, dividends to shareholders vary from quarter to quarter. They cannot be predicted in advance.

Security profits are the result of the sale of portfolio securities at prices higher than the prices at which they were bought. This is not a recurrent thing in the same sense as are the dividends that might be expected from a healthy individual corporation. They occur only when the mutual fund sells at a profit a security it owns. If the fund does not sell a single portfolio security during a year, there could be no security profit. If management felt impelled to show a security profit every year because the shareholders expected it, they would be restricted in their judgment. They would feel forced to sell some securities at a profit on some occasions when it would be better for all concerned if they were to hold those securities. Suppose the market as a whole were to decline for three or four years in a row. And suppose *all* the portfolio securities of a particular fund were affected. There might be no way of selling anything at a profit—and there might be no security profits, only losses.

Some fund managements believe that it is in the best interests of their shareholders to take profits when they can, subject to stated invest-ment objectives. Other managements believe in a "buy and hold" philosophy (again subject to stated investment objectives) that dictates very few sales and, therefore, very occasional security profits.

The main point of this section is that security profits are in a class completely different from the normal income picture. They are a "when occurring" item. In one sense, they are a return of capital to the investor. In no way can they be considered as income.

Misrepresenting the Return

It will be considered materially misleading hereafter for sales litera-ture—

(b)(2) *To represent or imply an assurance that an investor will receive a stable, continuous, dependable, or liberal return or that he will receive any specified rate or rates of return.*

Note particularly the word *imply*. A representative

Cannot assure or imply a *stable* return . . .

Cannot assure or imply a *continuous* return . . .

Cannot assure or imply a *dependable* return . . .

Cannot assure or imply a *liberal* return . . .

Cannot assure or imply a *specified rate* of return . . .

This clause, while easy enough to understand, still contains some traps.

In a burst of enthusiasm that is brought on by his own very real belief in the quality of his product, Mr. Eager Beaver makes this statement: "And just look at this record, Mr. Williams! This fund has paid a dividend every single quarter for the last 20 years . . . and the dividend has averaged four per cent over the past 15 years on a basis of reinvested security profits. Wouldn't you like to be receiving those dividend checks?"

Maybe not a deliberate violation on Mr. Beaver's part, but a very definite and serious violation, just the same. True, he has not said that the dividends were the *same* every quarter, he has not said the dividends were *liberal* in any way, and he has made no definite statement about results to be expected in the future. But he has very clearly *implied* by his choice of words that Mr. Williams can expect "*continuous, dependable*" return at a "*rate*" of four per cent, if he invests. Mr. Williams is being told very clearly (as far as he is concerned) that he can expect to receive a dividend check every quarter—of a fairly *stable* amount. He cannot, however, because there is no assurance that he will, and the fund management does not receive fixed income on which it can draw in order to guarantee such a thing to Mr. Williams. The error lies in failing to point out clearly that the dividends *vary* from quarter to quarter, that *no minimum* amount can be assured, and that *past* performance cannot be taken to mean *future* performance.

Let's see how Mr. Wiseman would make a statement about the dividend record of the fund.

"Here, Mr. Williams, is the lifetime record of this Fund. You can see here the year-to-year variation in the asset value of each share, as well as the dividends paid each year and the security profits that were distributed. In looking at the changes in net asset value, you should take into account the security profits, because those were a return of capital to the investor. Now, this dividend record looks excellent, doesn't it? But please note that the dividends varied from year to year, and they will vary in the future. In this type of investment, there can be no guarantee of the amount of the dividends, as I'm sure you realize.

"This is a completely different type of investment from that which guarantees your principal and a fixed rate of return. You exchange these guarantees in return for growth possibilities that are not present in guaranteed investments. The growth shown here for the past was obtained during a period of inflation and generally rising security prices . . . it could be more or less in the coming years."

Mr. Wiseman not only does not *imply* any assurance of fixed or minimum dividends in the future, he goes out of his way to state that they *have varied* in the past and that they *will vary* in the future. He carefully defines the relationship of security profits to net asset values and income. He contrasts the very *type* of investment involved with that of bonds and bank accounts.

Implying Preservation or Gain of Capital

It will be considered materially misleading hereafter for sales literature—

(c) *To represent or imply an assurance that an investor's capital will increase or that purchase of investment company shares involves a preservation of original capital and a protection against loss in value. To discuss accumulation of capital, preservation of capital, accumulation of an estate, protection againt loss of purchasing power, diversification of investments, financial independence or profit possibilities without pointing out or explaining the market price risks inherently involved in the investment.*

Section (c) has two parts. The first sentence says that it cannot be stated or implied that a purchase of shares of any mutual fund will result in an increase in the purchaser's capital, or that it will hold his capital at an even level, or even that it will protect him against loss.

All investors remember the precipitous decrease in the asset value in almost any mutual fund share in 1957 and 1962. There was a loss in net asset value per share of as much as 25 per cent in some funds in those years. This drop in value was over and above any sales charge deduction from the original investment, of course.

The moral behind these large drops in value is that shares of investment companies can never be purchased for any short-term investment. To do so would be to misunderstand their purpose and place in the financial picture. Actions and reactions on the stock market over the short-term are so completely unpredictable as to make it dangerous for a person to invest a sum in investment company shares that he might need within a short time.

Any prediction as to the long-range outlook would not be truly a prediction but rather an observation based on the long-term expectations of the American economy. *If* there is continued inflation and erosion of the dollar, and *if* the economy continues its growth as it has in the past, then it would seem apparent that an investment in a cross section of American industry should, over the long term, produce good results.

The second sentence of section (c) makes the point that regardless of the investment ideas discussed between an investor and a representative, there are always certain market risks built into mutual funds. Like any other investment, a mutual fund fluctuates in value along with the fluctuations in value of its portfolio securities. The decline or appreciation of all funds are, of course, not at the same rate as the market or as each other. At any time, there may also be some funds that run counter to the general trend of the securities market.

Any consideration of the advantages or the possibilities of gain should be balanced against the risks or possibilities of loss.

Federal Registration Explained

It is customary and normal for the point to be made that a mutual fund is registered under the Federal Investment Company Act of 1940. Such a statement is in the prospectus. But this statement alone might mislead an investor into believing that the registration referred to had something to do with supervising the investments of the fund. This, of course, is not true. Therefore, section (d) of the Statement of Policy says:

It will be considered materially misleading hereafter for sales literature—

> (d) *To make any reference to registration or regulation of any investment company under Federal or state authority without explaining that this does not involve supervision of management investment practices or policies.*

The explanation must be along these lines:

"Federal registration does not involve supervision of investment practices or policies."

"This does not imply any supervision of investment management or policy."

The Custodian's Function

In general, people have a great deal of confidence in banks. Much of this confidence stems from the strict regulations under which banks operate. To protect the public from the possibilities of out-right embezzlement or improper handling of the portfolio securities, the law requires bonding of fund employees and the physical custodianship of the fund's assets by a bank or trust company, a company which is a member of a national securities exchange, or the registered investment company itself. Most fund custodians are banks.

Physical custodianship is all that is required of the custodian in matters relating to the portfolio. Any other duties of the custodian such as paying out of dividends, acting as transfer agent, and the like are purely mechanical. *The custodian has nothing whatsoever to say about investment policies* and does not in any sense act in the same manner toward fund investors as though it were exercising a normal trusteeship. Section (e) expressly forbids the implication or representation that the custodian can protect the investor against possible depreciation in assets, or that it acts in any other capacity than those just mentioned.

It will be considered materially misleading hereafter for sales literature—

(e) *To represent or imply that services of banking institutions as custodian of securities, transfer agent, or dividend disbursing agent, provide protection for investors against possible depreciation of assets or that such institutions maintain any supervisory function over management in such matters as purchase and sale of portfolio securities or payment of dividends or provides any trusteeship protection, or to fail to state the extent of the limited role of the custodian whenever the advantages of custodial services are discussed.*

Under "INTERPRETATIONS" in the NASD's *What You Must Know . . .* the following appears:

Under Section (e) of the Statement of Policy, there is no objection to statements which say no more than "the XYZ Bank is custodian," or "the cash and securities of the investment company are held in custody of the XYZ Bank as custodian." But everything beyond these statements requires an explanation of the limited role of the bank as required by Section (e).

How Much Are Shares Worth at Redemption?

It will be considered materially misleading hereafter for sales literature—

(f) *To state or discuss the redemption features of investment company shares without explaining in such statement that the value of the shares on redemption may be more or less than the investor's cost, depending upon the market value of the portfolio securities at the time of redemption.*

Section (f) is a simple one. Mutual fund shares have a continuous market except in highly unusual circumstances. By law, an open-end fund must be ready to redeem its outstanding shares at the redemption value at any time.

Section (f) says that the redemption or liquidating value of shares may be discussed only if accompanied by a statement that this value may be more or less than the original cost to the investor.

Comparing a Fund with a Debt Security

It will be considered materially misleading hereafter for sales literature—

(g) (1) *To represent or imply that shares of an investment company are similar to or as safe as government bonds, insurance annuities, savings accounts or life insurance, or have the fixed income, principal, or any other features of a debt security.*

(2) *To represent or imply that the management of an investment company is under the same type of investment restrictions or is operated under limitations similar to or has fiduciary obligations such as those imposed by governmental authorities on savings banks and insurance companies, except to the extent that it is so restricted or limited by its statement of policy on file with this Commission.*

The difference between debt-type and equity investments are apparent as to safety of dollar principal and as to rates of return. Section (g) (1) just says that it cannot be indicated that one is like the other in any respect.

Insurance companies and banking institutions operate under very stringent regulations that dictate the types and amounts of investments they can make. They are required to carry certain reserves. Section (g) (2) says that it is misleading to represent or imply that the same type of regulations or restrictions apply to an investment company. The representative may, however, cite the limitations and restrictions that are imposed on any management by its own policy which is on file with the SEC and included in the prospectus.

Comparing with Another Security . . . or Investment . . . or Index or Average

It will be considered materially misleading hereafter for sales literature—

(h) *to use any comparison of any investment company security or medium of investment or any security index or average without pointing out—*

(1) *that the particular security or index or average and period were selected; and,*

(2) *that the results disclosed should be considered in the light of the company's investment policy and objectives, the characteristics and quality of the company's investments, and the period selected; and*

(3) *the material differences or similarities between the subjects of the comparisons; and,*

(4) *what the comparison is designed to show; and,*

(5) *anything else that may be necessary to make the comparison fair.*

Because of the difficulties involved in the clause *"anything else that may be necessary to make the comparison fair,"* any type of comparison of a fund's performance with anything else should not be made, unless that comparison has been supplied by the fund's underwriter.

It is an extremely difficult thing to make a fair comparison of any fund's performance with that of another fund very nearly akin to it, let alone to make a comparison with an average or an index. Different funds have different objectives, different fiscal years, different policies as to the taking of profits, and sometimes different managements at different periods of their history. An index or an average can't be said to have an "objective." An individual security on any basis is difficult to compare with a managed list of securities.

What You Must Know published by the NASD contains the following statements. They are quoted verbatim because of their importance.

Section (h) of the Statement of Policy requires that in comparisons of one investment company with another or with any other investment medium, the differences or similarities of the subjects compared must be made clear.

This section also requires that the purpose of the comparison be given. For example, if investment company shares were compared to savings bank deposits, it must be made clear that investment company shares are subject to market fluctuations and their dividends vary; whereas, savings bank deposits, although affording no opportunity for gain, are relatively safe and the interest paid thereon relatively stable. It would also be necessary to show that the purpose of the comparison was to point out the advantages of investment company shares in rising markets, or to keep pace with living costs, etc., and that the reverse would be true in periods of falling markets.

Any comparison which includes a chart or table that depicts the record of an investment company or illustrates results of assumed investments in the shares of an investment company must comply with the provisions of Section (j) as well as Section (h).

IMPORTANT—Any comparison of one investment company with another investment company not under the same management or sponsorship must be filed with the NASD in Washington for clearance before use.

2–106

Association members may not use published material that unfairly attacks ordinary life insurance and recommends the indiscriminate conversion of cash surrender values into proceeds for the purchase of investment company shares or other securities.

Several books, brochures, and reprints of published articles have been circulated for sale to securities dealers which support this proposition by misstatements, misinterpretations of fact, and dangerous and quite unqualified generalities. Dealers have been encouraged to use some of this material together with recommended form letters and advertising as a method of increasing securities sales.

Serious violations of the SEC's Statement of Policy on investment company sales literature can result from use of this material.

Much of the difficulty with this published material stems from efforts to oversimplify the actuarial basis of life insurance. This has resulted, among other things, in erroneous statements about cash surrender values and death benefits under life insurance policies on a level premium basis.

Indiscriminate representations to customers, as part of an overall general sales approach by a securities dealer, that ordinary life insurance is a "miserable investment" and that existing cash surrender values should be realized and the proceeds used to purchase mutual fund shares or other securities can have most undesirable results, both to the public interest and to the good name of the securities business.

Funds Are Not "New Capital" For Industry

It will be considered materially misleading hereafter for sales literature—

> *(i) To represent or imply that investment companies in general are direct sources of new capital to industry or that a particular investment company is such a source unless the extent to which such investments are made is disclosed.*

An already-issued security traded over-the-counter or on an exchange is a transaction only between the buyer and the seller. The company that issued the security does not enter into the purchase and sale at all, and none of the money handled goes to that company. Only when a company makes a *new* issue does it receive money into its treasury.

Because of this misconception, which is held by some people who are not familiar with the securities market, section (i) was written. Investment companies, in general, do not usually buy original issues. Their purchases are from other people or institutions who already own the securities. There are some funds which do invest in original issues from time to time. Section (i) permits the statement about new capital in regard to a specific fund when the statement includes the extent of this type of investment.

Problems in this area have been caused by misinterpretation of the catch-all phrase "investing in American industry." Some people, without giving sufficient thought to it, have misinterpreted this to mean that an investment in shares of any mutual fund means an investment in American industry in the sense that American industry *benefits* by such investment. It doesn't mean that. What it does mean is that the investor's money is invested in a part ownership of American corporations by purchase of such ownership from others—not from the corporations themselves. Thus, while such investments may benefit the investors, they do not contribute capital to business.

Performance Charts and Tables

Section (j) covers performance charts and tables. There are certain limitations and requirements to insure that the literature of all funds is represented in substantially the same manner. Under no circumstances can extracts be made from them. Either the whole chart or table should be shown or none at all. The smallest change or the underlining of any portion invalidates a chart or table.

Note the statement on such chart and tables when they are in supplemental literature—that is, in other than the prospectus. They all carry the legend:

This chart (or table, or brochure) *is authorized for distribution only if it is accompanied or preceded by an effective prospectus which gives the sales charges and other pertinent information.*

The Correct Word For Management

It will be considered materially misleading hereafter for sales literature—

(k) To make any extravagant claims regarding management ability or competency.

The very word *extravagant* implies deception. But like any word its meaning varies according to the way it is used and the emphasis placed on it. Terms like "expert" or comparative terms like "better," "smarter," and the like cannot be used. These words express an opinion—and it is the kind of opinion that cannot be backed by facts.

A Fund is Not a Cooperative

It will be considered materially misleading hereafter for sales literature—

(l) To represent or imply that investment companies are operated as, or are similar to, "co-operatives."

2–108

It is easy to fall into the innocent trap of believing that an investment company is like a cooperative. Quite frequently, an investor will reply to a representative's explanation of a fund, "Why, this is just like a co-op, isn't it?" Because it is *not* a cooperative, the investor will be misled if the representative says or implies that it is.

This false analogy is forbidden by Section (1) of the Statement of Policy because there are more points of difference between any mutual fund and a cooperative than there are points of similarity.

Fiduciaries and Investment Companies

It will be considered materially misleading hereafter for sales literature—

(*m*) *To represent or imply that investment company shares generally have been selected by fiduciaries.*

A fiduciary is anyone trusted with handling money or investments for another. Banks are fiduciaries. So are insurance companies and estate administrators. Section (m) does not forbid statements that a particular fund has been selected by certain specified fiduciaries if it has, but it *does* forbid such a statement as: "Banks use mutual funds for many of their trust accounts."

Dollar-Cost-Averaging*

This is a much used and much abused term used to describe a method of making fixed dollar investments at fixed intervals of time regardless of the price level of the shares being purchased. When properly handled, dollar-cost-averaging provides a mathematical certainty of buying, over a period of time, at an average cost that is less than the average price over that same period of time. But that is all it does do. In order to make it work, the same number of dollars must be invested at each interval selected over the time period, and no attention can be paid to the price as it varies from interval to interval. More shares are bought when prices are low than when prices are high. Even though this will then assure an average cost that is less than average price, it will not protect against loss in a declining market and it will certainly result in a loss if the investor discontinues such a plan when the value of his accumulated shares is less than the amount he has paid for them.

It is of special interest to the mutual fund industry because it is the basis on which many mutual fund shares are purchased. The important facts about it are:

---

* Dollar-cost averaging was discussed at length in Chapter 7 of Volume 1.

(1) It must be done automatically. The investor cannot try to outguess the market.

(2) The investor must keep it up even through extremely low price levels. Now since these usually occur during bad times, a person needs to be sure of his financial ability to do this before he starts such a plan.

(3) The investor must recognize that the method has only to do with average cost—that is, it cannot assure a profit, nor can it guarantee against a loss.

(4) If the investor must discontinue his plan when the market value of his shares is less than what he has paid, he will take a loss.

Bearing these things in mind, let's look at section (n) of the SOP.

It will be considered materially misleading hereafter for sales literature—

(*n*)(*1*) *To use the phrase "dollar averaging" or "averaging the dollar" (although the phrases "dollar cost averaging" or "cost averaging" are not objectionable) in referring to any plan of continuous investment in the shares of an individual investment company at stated intervals regardless of the price level of the shares.*

(2) *To discuss or portray the principles of dollar cost averaging, or cost averaging, or to discuss or portray any Periodic Payment Plan referred to in section 27 (a) of the Investment Company Act of 1940, without making clear—*

(i) *That the investor will incur a loss under such plan if he discontinues the plan when the market value of his accumulated shares is less than his cost; and*

(ii) *that the investor is investing his funds primarily in securities subject to market fluctuations and that the method involves continuous investment in such shares at regular intervals regardless of price levels; and*

(iii) *that the investor must take into account his financial ability to continue such plan through periods of low price levels; and*

(iv) *that such plans do not protect against loss in value in declining markets.*

(3) *To discuss or portray any other type of continuous investment plan without making clear that such type of investment plan does not assure a profit and does not protect against depreciation in declining markets.*

The terms "dollar averaging" or "averaging the dollar" cannot be used because they do not say what is meant. The plan deals with *cost* averaging, not *dollar* averaging. Therefore, a term that talks about cost averaging must be used—either "cost averaging" itself or "dollar cost averaging."

Section (n) (2) then goes on to say that the four things previously outlined in connection with this mathematical phenomenon must be stated. There should be no question as to *why* these things should be pointed out. They are *vital* to the investor's understanding and welfare.

Section (n) (2) has one additional important provision. It is that when discussing a Periodic Payment Plan (often referred to as a contractual, penalty, or front-end load plan) the *same* explanations must be given as those required in connection with dollar-cost-averaging.

The investor must constantly bear in mind that he is dealing with securities that are subject to fluctuations in value. In our history there have been many fairly lengthy periods of time in which security prices generally were declining. Because of such periods, and because of the fluctuations that are normal with such types of investments, no one can assure anybody at any time of a profit. Further, the possibility of loss must be explained and it must be stated in so many words that *no* plan can protect against depreciation in declining markets. Section (n)(3) just augments the previous two sections by making it mandatory that in *"any other"* type (the so-called "voluntary") of continuous investment plan discussed, the client or prospect must be told these two things—*no assurance of profit and no protection against loss in a declining market*.

The Sales Charge

There is a sales charge in connection with the purchase of fund shares. For information regarding these charges and other pertinent information, see the prospectus. These or similar statements appear on every piece of literature (other than the prospectus itself) that the representative handles. This is in conformance with section (o) of the SOP.

It will be considered materially misleading hereafter for sales literature—

> (o) *To fail to include in any sales literature which does not state the amount or rate of the sales commission (except communications which deal only with routine business matters or which do not purport to discuss or describe any investment company or investment company security) a clear reference to the prospectus or prospectuses for information concerning the sales commission, and other information.*

Switching a Security

There might be a few situations, comparatively speaking, in which an investor might be well-advised to switch his holding in one investment company into shares of another.

Section (p) states:

It will be considered materially misleading hereafter for sales literature—

(p) *To fail to include in any sales literature which is designed to encourage investors to switch from one investment company to another, or from one class of security of an investment company to another class, the substance of the following statement in a separate paragraph in type as large as that used generally in the body of the piece:*

> *Switching from the securities of one investment company to another, or from one class of security of an investment company to another, involves a sales charge for each such transaction, for details of which see the prospectus. The prospective purchaser should measure these costs against the claimed advantage of the switch.*

Comparing Fund Performance with Industry Performance

Section (q) is a comparison warning again. It should be apparent that the performance of a fund cannot be similar to the performance of an industry unless the portfolio is heavy enough in that industry and diversified enough within the same industry to make it so. It is problematical that any portfolio will act the same as a given industry, even for those funds that specialize in individual industries.

It will be considered materially misleading hereafter for sales literature—

(q) *To represent or imply that the performance of any particular company may be measured by or compared with or related to the performance of a particular industry unless the extent and scope of the portfolio of the particular company is such that its performance will generally approximate that of the industry.*

Use of Other Published Material

Much that is favorable to mutual funds has been written in recent years. An article that speaks of the funds in glowing terms tempts the representative to show it. Section (r) of the SOP forbids him from doing this, as it forbids him from showing comparative performances and figures from almost any book about mutual funds or investing.

It will be considered materially misleading hereafter for sales literature—

(*r*) *to employ material in whole or in part from published articles or documents descriptive of or relating to investment companies unless such material, or the literature including such material, complies with this Statement of Policy and in addition such material is not taken out of context in a manner which alters its intended meaning.*

Occasionally, *very* occasionally, a book or an article is written strictly in accordance with the Statement of Policy. Such books as *What About the Mutual Funds?* by John Straley were so written. Such material can be used. But in considering their use, one is always faced with the problem of determining which is usable and which is not. If the dealer does not already know, he can ask the NASD for a ruling. But even material that is prepared in accordance with the SOP must be used correctly. Under no circumstances should it be used out of context, if doing so will alter its meaning. Taking material out of context has the effect of changing its meaning or emphasis. For this reason, underlined material in a prospectus or supplemental literature is considered as material "out of context" because the underlined portions are emphasized at the expense of the portions not underlined.

REVIEW QUESTIONS

1. Describe "literature" as defined by the Statement of Policy.
2. Discuss periodic reports as sales literature.
3. Are communications between a representative and his employer classed as sales literature?
4. Explain how rate of return in percentage on investments in fund shares can legally be stated.
5. What is the most frequently violated section of the Statement of Policy?
6. Explain how the net performance of two funds might be quite similar although one had large realized capital gains and the other had none.
7. Can you logically combine dividends and realized capital gains in dollars and cents? In percentages? In any other way?
8. Why are mutual fund shares not a good short-term investment?
9. What is the custodian's relationship to a mutual fund?
10. When redemption features of fund shares are discussed, what *must* be stated?
11. Explain the difference between debt and equity investment.
12. What legal differences exist as between insurance companies and investment companies as to investments?
13. What are the five elements to be pointed out in comparisons?
14. What particular type of comparison requires special filing with the NASD?
15. What is the NASD's attitude about published material that attacks the life insurance industry?
16. What is meant by "direct sources of new capital"? Why are mutual fund purchases not generally such sources?
17. What can be said about the selection of mutual fund shares for investment by fiduciaries?
18. Is it a legal requirement that the sales charge be disclosed when discussing mutual fund shares?
19. Discuss "switching" and its effect on a shareholder's capital.
20. Under what circumstances can the performance of a fund be compared with a particular industry?

Chapter 7

Contractual
Plans

INTRODUCTION

Definition

A contractual plan is a plan for the accumulation of mutual fund shares. It is a plan with a specified *goal* because it calls for a *specified number of dollars* to be invested over a *specified period of time*. Most plans are sold on the expectation of regular monthly payments until the total amount of the plan has been paid in. On a monthly payments basis, plans vary in length from five years to as long as 17½ years, with the 10-year plan being the most common. It is because of the fixed number of payments to be made that the term *contractual* came into being.

Characteristic of the contractual plan is the manner in which the sales charge is deducted from plan payments. Generally, the major part of the sales charge for the entire plan is deducted from the first twelve monthly payments. Because of this, the contractual plan is frequently referred to as a *front-end load, front-load, penalty,* or *pre-paid charge* plan. This method of deducting charges in advance does not mean that the charges are more for the entire plan. As will be developed later, the total sales charge on larger completed plans is frequently less than the sales charge on the same amounts invested through "voluntary" plans. One type of contractual plan deducts the major part of the sales charge at lesser rates over the first three years' payments. Total sales charges for this plan approximate the sales charges for the same investment made through a voluntary plan.

Legally, a contractual plan is termed a *periodic payment plan* under Section 27 of the Investment Company Act of 1940.

Actually, a contractual plan is not contractual insofar as the investor is concerned. He states that he *intends* to complete the specified payments, but there is no contract that forces him to do so. He always owns whatever shares he has accumulated under the plan. Should he discontinue payments and liquidate, he may receive less than he paid, but he does not lose his actual equity.

The plan *is* contractual as far as the sponsor and the custodian are concerned, however. The terms of the plan cannot be changed at any time without the prior approval of the planholder. This is a one-sided contract, which can be very much to the advantage of the planholder. (See later discussion under "*Features*.") An unusual type of contractual plan was developed in 1966 in which there is no "front load." Sales charges are deducted in the same manner as in a voluntary plan, but the plan is contractual as to its other features.

History

The contractual plan is almost as old as the mutual fund, though the plans sold in the early thirties differed in some respects from those currently offered. Quite a number of the early plans were unable to meet the conditions imposed by the '40 Act and were discontinued. During the forties, there were only a few new plans offered. Growth in planholder accounts in the fifties was accompanied by growth in the number of plans offered. By the end of 1960, there were more than 40 different contractual plans registered. By the end of 1962 there were 50.

According to the Association of Mutual Fund Plan Sponsors, Inc., an organization of contractual plan distributors, there were some $1.6 billion already invested in planned investments (or almost eight per cent of all mutual fund assets combined at the end of 1962.). As of the same date, the Association reported that there remained almost $3.5 billion in payments to be made on currently outstanding plans.

Because of a continuously increasing number of dealers marketing such plans and because of the availability of such plans on an increasing number of funds, contractual plans have become a very significant factor in the growth of total investments in mutual funds. The SEC, however, as a part of changes in the '40 Act requested of the Congress in 1967, has asked for legislation to ban the contractual plan.

In discussing the number or amount of plan payments yet to be made on contractual plans, the question naturally arises as to how many of the agreed payments will actually be made. A study made in 1964 concerning the percentage of investors who complete or drop contractual plans has yielded interesting results.

The accounts of four major contractual sponsors were analyzed for the full payment period of their plans. Two of the plans were for 120 months, one was for 96 months, and the fourth was for 150 months or 12½ years.

The following is a direct quote from an address on April 29, 1964, by Rowland A. Robbins, president of the Association of Mutual Fund Plan Sponsors, Inc.:

"Of the 17,200 accounts opened, 9,400 (or 55%) were still in force after periods of 10 to 13 years. These showed an unrealized profit of $19.8 million.

"An additional 4,900 accounts (or 28%) had redeemed with profits of $5.4 million; these two categories accounting for 83% of all accounts opened.

"This leaves 2,900 accounts (or 17%) who redeemed with aggregate losses of $240,000, representing an average loss, per account, of approximately $80.

"Reverting to the 9,400 accounts still in force, 750 of these were still in the 1-to-12 payment category; yet against the $171,000 paid in, their accounts were worth $294,000.

"Another 469 had only made 13 to 24 payments. These paid in $354,000; yet their accounts were worth $587,000.

"Still another 335 had only made 25 to 36 payments. These paid in $398,000, yet were worth $672,000."

In other words, less than one contractual plan owner out of six redeemed, and then at an average loss of only $80. The 9,400 contractual plans still in effect showed an average gain for all accounts (both large and small) of over $2,300. As a group the net profits added up to $25,000,000 from redemptions or retained investments on invested payments of $42,000,000.

In examining and interpreting these figures, it must be borne in mind that all the plans began in the early and middle 1950s, just at the time that a great bull market was beginning. All four plans thus were able to take advantage of the rise in stock values, and all four suffered declines in the set-backs of 1957, 1960, and 1962. The statistics quoted are the direct result of what happened to the investors' dollars during that period. Had any other time span been studied, of course, different percentages and dollar increases or decreases would have been shown.

Features

Accumulation Plans (*voluntary*) and Open Accounts were discussed in Chapter 3. Features of the contractual plan here discussed refer to those features that are *different from* or *in addition to* the features of fund share ownership and voluntary accumulation plans.

(1) **It is a PLAN.** Unlike any other form of accumulation "plan," the contractual plan *is a Plan.* It has a definite goal—a fixed number of dollars to be invested. It has a method for reaching the goal—a fixed number

of investments at regular intervals in fixed amounts. By following the plan, an investor puts a predetermined number of dollars into his program within a predetermined length of time.

(2) **Incentive.** Innumerable jokes about New Year's resolutions point out that intentions do not necessarily mean action. Most people require an incentive to bolster their good intentions. This is provided by the contractual plan in the *built-in loss.* Because a large part of the total sales charge for the entire program usually is deducted from the first twelve monthly payments, the planholder is placed in a potential loss position during the early years of his plan. He must continue his payments. If his plan is to succeed— *he can't afford to stop.* The persistence rate of investments by planholders mentioned earlier in this chapter shows the degree of effectiveness of this feature.

(3) **Insurance.** Mortgage insurance, a policy designed to leave the home free and clear in case of the death of the breadwinner, has become increasingly popular in recent years. "Self-completion" insurance is like mortgage insurance in that it assures the completion of a plan. It is available with most contractual plans in most states in which they may be sold. A few "voluntary" plans can be covered with this type of insurance, but the rates are somewhat higher than those for the contractual plans. The insurance offered with the contractual plans is the low-cost insurance known as "group, reducing term." Premiums are paid only on the payments yet to be made on the plan. If the planholder dies, the insurance company immediately completes the plan payments. With most plans, a maximum of $30,000 in insurance can be obtained or the equivalent of coverage of a $250 a month, 10-year plan.

(4) **Guaranteed charges.** It was stated earlier that the contractual plan was a one-sided contract. The plan sponsor guarantees that the sales charge will not be changed during the life of the plan. Also, the sponsor guarantees that the custodian charges will remain the same. This is a very important feature in these days of rising costs.

The contractual plan sponsor guarantees the planholder against rising accounting costs in exchange for the use of the money received from planholders in the form of prepaid charges. The underwriters of fund voluntary plans cannot offer such a guarantee because they have no "advance" money that can be put to work to offset rising costs to them.

IMPORTANT: While the guarantees as to charges are important, it is equally important to note that most contractual plans have "custodian fees" that may be completely absent from voluntary plans.

(5) **Reinvestment at NAV.** As discussed in the chapter on the mutual fund prospectus, some open accounts and some voluntary accumulation plans reinvest dividends at net asset value while others reinvest at offering price. It is characteristic of contractual plans that dividends are reinvested at net asset value. Over a period of years, this a distinct advantage

to the planholder. Some funds have voluntary plans in which dividends are reinvested at offering price and, at the same time, have contractual plans in which dividends are reinvested at net asset value.

(6) **Lower sales charge.** For large plans, typically of $100 a month or more, the sales charge for the completed plan is frequently considerably less than it would be for an equivalent investment through a voluntary plan at the same rate over the same length of time. In effect, the larger contractual plans are long-term "letters of intent." For example, an investor putting $200 a month into a voluntary plan might have a sales charge of 8½ per cent applied against each payment. If he continued for 10 years, he would have bought $24,000 worth of shares at offering price. On the other hand, through a contractual plan, his total sales charge would have been only 7 per cent of the $24,000 instead of 8½ per cent. Again, custodian fees or charges on both types of plans for a particular fund's shares must be checked to see whether there is, in fact, a true savings in total charges.

(7) **Partial liquidation.** When an investor has purchased fund shares outright or through an open account or "voluntary" accumulation plan, he either holds share certificates or shares are held by the custodian for his account, or both. Should he liquidate any of those shares, he has completed a transaction. That is, should he wish to buy the shares back at a later date, he would have to do so on the basis that it was an entirely new purchase at the then effective sales charge. On liquidation, he might receive more or less than he had paid for the shares; on repurchase, he might pay more or less than the price he received on liquidation.

Many contractual plans allow the planholder to make a partial liquidation (usually up to 90 per cent of his accumulated shares) after he has made a certain number of payments into the plan. He is then permitted to buy back the same number of shares for his plan account *without sales charge*. Again, he may receive more or less than he paid on liquidation, and he may pay more or less for the new shares he buys. However, he buys at *net asset value*, not at the offering price. It is important to check each plan prospectus to get details of this feature. Some plans allow the repurchase of the same number of *shares*, and some allow the reinvestment of the same number of *dollars* as received on partial liquidation. Some permit the withdrawal of shares (instead of liquidation) and permit the replacement of an equal number of shares (again at net asset value). The frequency of such liquidations or withdrawals and replacement is restricted in most cases. Note that a partial liquidation involves a sale as far as taxes are concerned. Because there may be a capital gain or a capital loss, the investor must note such gain or loss on his annual tax statement. The tax base of the plan itself must be changed to account for this when final liquidation is made after completion of the plan.

(8) **Tax savings.** Some, but not all, of the contractual plans operate under a ruling of the Treasury Department that allows all of the plan-

holders to be treated as an "association taxable as a corporation for Federal income tax purposes." So long as the custodian fees and the administrative expenses for supervising the plan accounts exceed, as a whole, the income received (from the underlying fund shares) for all of the planholders, the *distributions* are considered a return of capital to the planholders.

Whether they are received in cash or in shares, they are non-reportable for tax purposes. Such distributions do, however, go to reduce the cost of the plan in determining long-term gain or loss on liquidation of the plan. While this treatment does save in *current* taxes, it does not necessarily follow that it will save in *ultimate* taxes if the plan is liquidated. The overall effect will depend upon such things as the investor's tax bracket during the accumulation period and his probable tax bracket at the termination of the plan. It will also depend upon whether the plan is liquidated outright, liquidated through a periodic withdrawal plan over a period of years, or is held until death.

Details as to the reporting of distributions will be found in the prospectus of each plan.

THE PLAN PROSPECTUS

This section of the text should be studied in conjunction with the current prospectus of any contractual plan.

Note that a contractual plan has a *plan* or *investment plan* prospectus to offer itself. It is not a share prospectus of the type described in Chapter 5.

Page One

On page one of the prospectus is a lead-off statement similar to the following:

"Three types of . . . . PLANS are offered for the accumulation of shares of . . . . FUND, Inc."

This is followed by a statement as to the identity of the *sponsor* or underwriter of the plans.

There then follows an explanation of charges for *Single Payment Plans*, for *Systematic Investment Plans*, and for *Systematic Investment Plans with Insurance*. (This last one is omitted from prospectuses offering plans in states that do not allow insurance as a part of the plan.)

The breakdown of percentage charges in made on three different bases:

(1) the range, maximum to minimum, of the "creation and sales charge" to the total amount of the plan;

(2) the range, maximum to minimum, of the same charge to the net amount invested; and

(3) the range, maximum to minimum of the "total deductions" to the net amount invested.

These statements should be contrasted with the simple statement of offering price required on page one of a share prospectus.

Following the general statements of charges, there is usually a statement of the *length* of the plan, such as ". . . Plans call for regular monthly payments for 10 years." Some plans are available for different periods; some offer a choice of 10- or 15-year, others offer different alternates, some offer more than two different periods.

While not necessarily in the following order, the first page will also contain:

(1) A statement that the payments, after deduction of authorized charges, are applied to the purchase of the underlying fund shares at net asset value.

(2) The warning that because a major part of the (creation and) sales charge is deducted from the first year's payment, withdrawal or termination in the early years will probably result in a loss. This warning is emphasized by a statement of the percentage ratio of total charges to payments made at the end of the first six months, at the end of the first year, and at the end of the second year. This portion differs for certain plans that deduct 20 per cent of payments for the first two years and 10 per cent the third year for sales charges. Also, it differs as to the type of plan without prepaid charges.

(3) An explanation that the plans are intended for long-term investment purposes and are not suitable for quick profits or for those unable to continue their payments to completion.

(4) The four warnings that make up section (n)(2) of the Statement of Policy that are required whenever "periodic payment plans" are discussed.

(5) A statement that direct purchases of the underlying Fund shares can be made, giving the maximum sales charge involved and including the phrase *"without penalties for early termination."*

(6) A statement that *"prepayment of all or any of the first 12 (or 13) payments results in a smaller investment in fund shares . . . than would result from a direct investment of the same amount. Such prepayment increases the possibilities of loss in the event of early termination."*

(7) Some sponsors point out that the investment advisor of the underlying mutual fund receives compensation for its services to the fund, and the cost of these services, together with other operating expenses of

the fund, are deducted from the fund's net income prior to the distribution of its dividends to its shareholders.

No SEC Approval

As with the fund prospectus itself, and with all other prospectuses, this first page must carry the statement required under Rule 425 "THESE SECURITIES HAVE NOT BEEN APPROVED OR DISAPPROVED etc." In addition, the following must appear:

THIS PROSPECTUS IS VALID ONLY WHEN ACCOMPANIED BY THE CURRENT......................FUND PROSPECTUS.

Some plan prospectuses have the fund prospectus bound with it in the same booklet. Others do not. In any event, a representative must use both prospectuses in presenting a plan.

Table of Contents

A table of contents, listing the major sections of the prospectus, usually appears inside the cover page. There may also be a specific notation that

"No salesman, dealer, or other person is authorized by the XYZ Sponsor or the XYZ Fund to give any information or to make any representation other than those contained in this Prospectus or the Prospectus of the XYZ Fund or in any other printed or writteen material issued over the name of the Sponsor or the Fund, and no person is entitled to rely upon any information not contained herein or therein."

The Plans

Page two usually contains a brief description of each type of plan, how an investor may purchase his plan, and the proper way to maintain it. There is usually some reference in this section to the investment objective of the fund whose shares form the basis for the plans.

Single payment investment plans are for a single lump sum investment (similar to an outright purchase of fund shares), for which there is a single sales charge often the same as the charge for an outright fund share purchase. The minimum amount is specified. In most cases, the plans are issued only in multiples of $100 above the minimum. Frequently, a separate prospectus is issued that offers only the single payment plan . . . this is generally for use in the few states that do not permit regular contractual plans.

The question may arise as to whether it is better for the investor to make a lump sum investment in the form of an outright purchase of shares of the fund or in the form of a single payment investment plan. If he wishes his dividends and security profits in the form of shares, he may be better off with the single payment. If he wishes to receive dividends in cash, he might be better off with the outright purchase of shares. Should an investor wish the privilege of partial liquidation and replacement discussed earlier, he might prefer a single payment plan to an outright purchase of shares.

The investor must carefully check the rights and privileges of the holder of a single payment investment plan against the corresponding rights and privileges of a fund shareholder. Here he must take into account any difference in sales charge and any charges that may be made by the custodian or others against the plan.

Systematic Investment Plans are next described in somewhat more detail than that given on page one. This section often contains special features that are peculiar to the plans offered, i.e. that are not common to other contractual plans. It should be studied carefully.

Charts

There are three types of charts in the plan prospectus. They are not necessarily in the same order in each prospectus, but each of the following is shown:

(1) A chart that shows the distribution of charges on the minimum plan offered, in dollars and cents and as a percentage, for the full duration of the plan, for the first six months, for the first year, and for the first two years. The number of payments will usually show up as one more than the number of months for the periods short of the full plan. This is because the first payment is usually double the amount of the monthly payment specified. This particular chart is intended to show the investor that he will be in a very poor position during the early stages of the plan.

(2) A chart that shows the charges, the "break points," and the net investments in shares of single payment plans. Percentages of charges to total payment and to net investment are also shown.

(3) Charts that give all charges on each systematic investment plan offered, with and without insurance. These show the allocation of payments and deductions for each plan.

Rights and Privileges

Either with or just after the charts, is a section on the rights and privileges of planholders. These spell out the items listed earlier in this chapter under *Features*. There are certain things to look for under each of the headings.

Dividends. Under a heading that usually reads "Dividends and Distributions" is an explanation of how these are handled under the particular plan. This section will show whether distributions are automatically credited in shares, whether there is any charge for the reinvestment of dividends, and whether or not the planholder has the right to receive his distributions in cash. Some plans *require* that dividends and distributions be taken in the form of additional shares in the plans. If this feature is optional, it is not advantageous for the investor to receive the cash. If his purpose in starting the plan is the accumulation of shares, he will get *share-compounding* by leaving his dividends and distributions in the plan. Note that the term *compounding* by itself and the term *dollar-compounding* are properly used only with interest-bearing accounts such as bank accounts. The correct term is share-compounding, because it is the share themselves which are compounded.

Beneficiary. Under a heading such as "Designation of Beneficiary" is a statement as to how the plan may be registered to provide for transfer of ownership, without the need for probate, on the death of the planholder.

There are marked differences in tax liabilities, in ownership, and in planholder's rights between different forms of trusts (e.g. revocable and irrevocable). Unless the purchaser has a lawyer's familiarity with the effects of the different forms of trusts (e.g. revocable and irrevocable), he should not adopt any form of trust without consultation with his attorney.

Partial Withdrawals. If the plan allows partial withdrawals or partial liquidations, the provisions will be detailed in this section. There are marked differences between different contractual plans in the rights to make partial withdrawals or liquidations. Particular differences are usually found in the provisions as to restoration of *dollars* or of *shares*, if restoration after withdrawal is permitted. The basic differences in different plans is:

(1) Some plans do not allow partial withdrawal or liquidation.

(2) Some plans permit partial liquidation, but do not permit replacement of money or shares.

(3) Some plans permit partial liquidation with the provision that the dollar amount may be reinvested in additional shares at net asset value after all regular plan payments have been completed. While such plans may allow partial liquidations to be made more than once during the progress of the plan and may allow replacement of the proceeds in "installments," they may allow no more than the equivalent of one "round trip."

(4) Some plans, particularly the more recent ones, originally allowed an unlimited number of partial liquidations or partial withdrawals and replacements therefor until such time as the plan was *terminated*. Note that *terminated* is not the same as *completed*. A plan is *completed* when all of the agreed payments have been made. A plan is *terminated* when the plan certificate is surrendered in return for complete liquidation or for share certificates.

Because of "in and out" transactions by a number of planholders who were using this feature solely to speculate, most plans now restrict the frequency of partial liquidations and replacements. Such restrictions still permit the emergency liquidations that were originally contemplated when this feature was first introduced.

Those plans permitting partial withdrawals usually have a provision that a certain number of payments must have been made before the withdrawal can be made. Also, there is a limitation as to the amount of such withdrawal. Commonly, a partial liquidation will not be made in amounts less than $50 nor more than 90 per cent of the total accumulated shares. Here again, each prospectus must be individually checked. There are wide variations in these provisions.

Transfer. Rights as to transfer or assignment are detailed here. Generally, the right of assignment extends to banks or other lending institutions so that the planholder may use the accumulated shares in his plan as collateral for a loan. There is usually a custodian charge for a transfer or assignment, including a Declaration of Trust filed after the application for the plan, and there may be transfer taxes to be paid by the planholder.

Termination. The planholder has the right to terminate his plan at any time. He may deliver his certificate in exchange for his accumulated shares or he may receive the proceeds of liquidation of his shares, at his option. There may be a custodian charge for termination before completion of the plan.

It is this ability to terminate the plan at any time that makes it no real contract on the part of the investor.

IMPORTANT: Termination in the early years will almost certainly result in a loss to the planholder. Therefore, it ordinarily is to the planholder's advantage that he not request early termination. Even when a planholder can terminate and receive more money than he actually paid into the plan, he may be doing himself a disservice. He is forfeiting the prepaid sales charge on shares he has not yet purchased, and the difference between his liquidating value and his actual payments may be less than he would have received from some other form of investment. Should the planholder need money he should consider his partial liquidation privileges and the collateral value of his plan for a bank loan.

Receipts, Notices and Reports. Details are given under this heading as to what information will be sent to planholders. While all plans call for audited reports and current prospectuses of the underlying fund to be sent to planholders, not all handle "notices of payment due" in the same form. Some send the notice as a part of, or together with, the receipt for the last payment. Others send a notice of payment due separately from the receipt. In some cases, delinquency notices are sent when a payment has been missed. In other cases, such notices are not sent until several payments have been missed.

Default and Reinstatement. Except in the case of insured plans, the major effect of missed payments is to delay completion of the plan. Sponsors generally consider a plan to be in default when a payment is not made on or before the due date, but this has no effect on the shares already bought by the planholder. Usually, the sponsor reserves the right to terminate a plan when it is in default for a year or more. When a plan is so terminated, the planholder is issued a share certificate for his accumulated shares, plus a check for the value of any fractional share.

Meetings and Voting Rights. Provisions under this section are quite generally similar in all plans. A planholder has all the rights of the fund shares held for his account that any other fund shareholder has.

Advance Payments. Most plans have provisions for accepting payments in advance of the regular schedule, usually in multiples of the specified monthly payment. In some cases, there is a reduction in custodian charges when advance payments are made, but there is no reduction in sales charge, of course.

Sales and Service Charges

In addition to the charts that appear earlier in the prospectus, there is a section that describes the various charges on minimum plans (i.e. it describes the maximum charges). This section also spells out the obligations of the plan sponsor and custodian in return for the fees they charge. If there is a custodian fee for maintaining an account after the plan has been completed, the details are given here.

Plan Completion Insurance

Provisions under this section vary widely from plan to plan. One thing all of the insurance policies have in common is that the proceeds are to be paid to the custodian for the specific purpose of completing plan payments. The proceeds are not paid to the estate or to any beneficiary as they are in the insurance programs of some "voluntary" plans.

An insured plan places an obligation on the planholder's estate to complete the plan payments. The purpose of the insurance is to meet that obligation. The obligation must exist to make it possible for the insurance to be issued.

The incontestability features and the requirements as to physical examinations should be checked. While there are "standard" and "sub-standard" rates applied, the risk must be satisfactory to the insurance companies before the insurance will be issued. Note also that the plan will not be placed into effect until after acceptance by the insurance companies. If the insurance application is rejected, most plans are automatically issued as plans without insurance. This is generally stated on the application form for the plan.

Tax Status

For Federal income tax purposes, the sponsor, the custodian and all the planholders are treated as an association, taxable as a corporation.

The custodianship, which is registered under the Investment Company Act of 1940 as a unit investment trust, usually elects to comply with the requirements of Subchapter M of the Internal Revenue Code and files, for Federal income tax purposes, as a regulated investment company pursuant to section 851 of the Internal Revenue Code. Thus, the unit investment trust is not subject to Federal income tax, on otherwise taxable income, to the extent of the dividends or distributions paid to the investors.

The custodian sends a yearly notice to the investors which contains the amount and nature of any income taxable to him. The notice is usually sent simultaneously with the yearly capital gain distribution notice, if the unit investment trust is on a calendar year tax base.

A statement is required in this section of the prospectus that dividends or capital gain distributions received by the investor shortly after his purchase of a contractual plan, although in effect a return of capital, may be subject to Federal income tax.

Underlying Fund

The short description of the shares of the underlying mutual fund (and the rights and privileges of its shareholders) appearing in this section refers to the accompanying or attached fund prospectus for full information. Usually, there is another statement that the shares of the fund may be purchased in a voluntary accumulation account. If the underlying fund is one of a group handled by the same management company, the conversion and exchange privileges within the group are enumerated.

Monthly Withdrawal Plans

Many sponsors allow purchasers of single payment plans and owners of completed periodic payment plans to make monthly withdrawals on a regular basis. The purposes and uses of withdrawal plans are discussed in the next chapter.

Substitution of Shares

No matter how secure the underlying fund may be, there is always the remote possibility that due to a change in franchise agreement, management contract or other unknown factors, the sponsor of the contractual plans will deem it advisable to substitute the shares of another investment medium or mutual fund as the underlying investment for the contractual plan.

This action cannot take place without the consent of the custodian (in some cases written notice to the custodian of the sponsor's intention is the only requirement) and without giving written notice of the proposed substitution to each investor. A reasonable description of the new fund shares is given, and the investor is granted the option to terminate his plan if he does not agree to the substitution. If the investor agrees to the substitution, he automatically agrees to bear his pro rata cost of the expense and taxes incurred. Of course, no change which affects an investor can be made without his consent.

Similarly, a new custodian may also be substituted after notice has been sent to the investor giving him the same option to terminate the plan.

In the unlikely event that fund shares cannot be purchased for a specified period of time, and neither the sponsor nor the custodian has selected a substitute investment medium or mutual fund, the custodian is authorized without further action to proceed with full termination of the contractual plan.

GENERAL INFORMATION

Custodian

This section includes a description of the custodian, its organization and its agreement with the sponsor. Under the Investment Company Act, the custodian must be a bank or trust company having an aggregate capital, surplus, and undistributed profit of at least one-half million dollars, although in practice most sponsors have requirements of from $1 to $3 million. The custodian may not resign its custodianship on plans already in force, even after the custodianship agreement has terminated, unless a successor custodian has been designated and has accepted the custodianship. A custodian agreement cannot be amended in any way which might affect the rights and privileges of an investor, without first obtaining his written consent.

The custodian maintains physical custody of the assets of the contractual plans, which are the actual shares of the underlying mutual fund.

The custodian's duties are to receive the investor's monthly payments and apply them to the purchase of the underlying fund shares at net asset value, after making the deductions authorized in the prospectus and plan certificates. The custodian also:

(a) receives the dividends and capital gain distributions on the underlying fund shares, and either remits them to the investors or credits them in the form of additional fund shares for the investors' accounts;

(b) liquidates contractual plans either completely or in part;

(c) maintains the records vital to each investor's account;

(d) mails each investor a receipt and reminder notice for each payment;

(e) mails delinquency notices, when necessary;

(f) mails notices including distribution notices, tax statements and other reports to investors; and

(g) mails and tabulates proxy solicitation material which is provided by the sponsor.

Should the sponsor fail to have the required periodic audits made of the custodian's records, the custodian is then obligated to arrange for such audits. Additionally, the custodian must prepare and file other reports required by law.

As in the case of the custodian of the underlying mutual fund shares, the custodian of the contractual plan (which may or may not be the same custodian) makes no representation as to the enforceability of the plans or of the fund shares and has no responsibility for the investment policies and practices of the fund managers, for the choice of insurance carriers, or for the acts or omissions of the insurance carriers or of the terms of the insurance policies. The custodian is not responsible for registration or qualification of the securities under Federal or state law, or any rule or regulation thereunder, and is liable only for its own willful misconduct or gross negligence.

Sponsor (The Plan Company)

A statement covering the sponsor's date of incorporation, the state in which it is incorporated, and that it is a registered broker-dealer and a member of the National Association of Securities Dealers, Inc., usually precedes the listing of the individual principal officers and directors of the sponsor. This listing shows the titles and business history for the past five years of every principal officer and director.

All employes and officers of the sponsor must be bonded and a statement outlining the details of the bond appears.

There is often a relationship between the sponsor of the plan and the underwriter of the fund and/or the fund manager. If there is any such relationship, it is described. If there is any relationship, ownership of, or agreement with any brokerage firm, insurance company, or bank, it must be stated along with complete disclosure of the ownership of the sponsor corporation.

Should the sponsor, or its officers or directors, have any connection with a brokerage firm which has received commissions from the underlying mutual fund, the amount of such commissions on securities transactions for the fund must be stated.

General

Either in this section or the preceding one, disclosure must be made of how the plans are sold (whether exclusively by one or more broker-dealers or by independent broker-dealers with signed selling agreements) together with a statement of the range of the sales commissions reallowed the authorized investment brokers and mutual fund dealers from the sales charge paid by the investor. If the sponsor has a special bonus or incentive arrangement, it too, must be indicated.

This section usually includes all information too brief to warrant its own heading and contains a statement that the plans were organized under and are governed by a specific state law as a unit investment trust under the Investment Company Act of 1940 and are so registered with the Securities and Exchange Commission—and that such registration does not imply supervision of management or investment practices or policies by the Securities and Exchange Commission or any other governmental agency.

It is also in this section that the sponsor usually states the total agreed payments which it has registered with the Securities and Exchange Commission. Counsel for the sponsor will also generally render an opinion as to the legality of the plans.

The prospectus, of necessity, is an abbreviated document. Certain information required in the registration statement is omitted and certain agreements are merely referred to in passing. All of these documents, in their entirety, are filed as exhibits with the registration statement and are available for public scrutiny in Washington, D.C. A statement to this effect appears in the prospectus.

There is one last item of major importance: the list of states in which the various types of plans are qualified for sale. Because of the legal requirements of individual states, contractual plans have to be individually registered in each state (under its "Blue Sky" laws) in which the sponsor wishes to offer the plans. Some states will not allow any contractual plan to be offered and sold, some states will not allow insured plans to be sold, and the sponsor may not have made application in others.

Hypotheticals

These are tables of assumed investments. The accumulation period shown is either the length of the plan or the life of the fund, whichever is the shorter. These tables must be made in accord with the requirements of section (j) of the Statement of Policy.

The number of these hypothetical tables shown varies from plan to plan. A minimum plan (the minimum face amount) for the shortest length of time offered, with the highest percentage of charges, must be shown. Many sponsors also show a $50 per month plan, a $100 per month plan, and larger plans, with or without the assumption of a year down-payment.

Of course these hypotheticals show past history only and are no assurance of future performance, but they can be used with the appropriate hedges by a potential investor to see what would have happened to his payments and what their liquidating value would have been had he taken out a contractual on the date indicated and made his payments regularly. The important thing to remember is that these tables, like the charts shown in the mutual fund literature, show past history only and there is always the possibility that the fund may not be as successful in the future and that different market conditions may exist.

Financial Statements

The last part of the prospectus traditionally contains an opinion rendered by independent public accountants concerning the financial condition of the unit investment trust (the contractual plan itself as distinguished from the plan sponsor). This accompanies a Statement of Condition of the property held by the custodian (sometimes also called Statement of Assets and Liabilities) and the related Statements of Receipts and Disposition, Statement of Income, Expense and Disposition, and Statement of Shares Held by the Custodian (dating either for the last three years or from the inception of the trust).

If the unit investment trust has qualified under subchapter M of the Internal Revenue Code there is a statement explaining why no provision has been made for Federal Income Tax.

Application Forms

Sometimes the last pages in the prospectus contain an actual Application Form and Statement of Health (for insured plans).

REVIEW QUESTIONS

1. Define a contractual plan.
2. Is the contractual plan legally binding? On whom?
3. Discuss the contractual plan as a *plan*.
4. Describe the incentive feature of contractual plans.
5. What is the self-completion insurance feature of contractual plans?
6. Discuss guaranteed charges as a feature.
7. Compare partial liquidation in a contractual plan with partial liquidation in a voluntary plan.
8. What is the possible tax liability on partial liquidation?
9. What warning about the effect of the method of deducting sales charges is given on the cover or first page of a plan prospectus?
10. Describe single payment investment plans.
11. When might an outright purchase of mutual fund shares be better than a single payment investment plan?
12. What three types of charts of charges are found in a plan prospectus?

13. What is meant by "rights and privileges" of plan holders?
14. What is the difference between a "completed" plan and a "terminated" plan?
15. How is termination effected and what are the results of termination?
16. Discuss default and reinstatement.
17. How are advance payments treated in a plan?
18. Just what payment is made by the insurance company on proof of death of a plan-holder and to whom is it paid?
19. Discuss "substitution of shares."
20. What are the principal duties of a plan custodian?
21. State the authority, responsibility, and duties of a plan sponsor.
22. What are hypothetical tables?

Chapter 8

Withdrawal Plans

BACKGROUND

Definition

A withdrawal plan is a program which calls for the planned withdrawal of the dollars invested in a mutual fund, or of the shares themselves, over an extended period of time. Also called *level payment plans*, *check-a-month plans*, and *periodic remittance plans*, withdrawal plans all have many features in common.

A withdrawal plan involves the purchase of mutual fund shares. A minimum purchase of $5,000 or $10,000 is usually specified by most funds offering such plans. Upon purchase, an investor can specify a method of regular monthly or quarterly withdrawals.

Until July 1, 1964, it was difficult for mutual funds to convey the principles of withdrawal plans. Before that date, the Securities and Exchange Commission did not allow illustrations and tables of assumed investments in withdrawal plans such as were permitted for accumulation plans. It was thus exceedingly difficult to demonstrate just what an investor might expect from the plan, particularly regarding the problem of invasion of the original capital as payments were made from the fund.

The problem of capital invasion is the crux of any withdrawal plan because an investor, seeking regular withdrawals,

(1) May want to have a reasonable assurance that, if he must invade capital, he will not so depreciate the balance of the principal left in the fund that he runs the real risk of depleting his resources.

(2) May want to realize as high payments as possible within a limited time span without attempting to conserve his capital.

Flexibility

In general, most mutual funds provide two types of withdrawal plans. The more common calls for liquidation of varying full and fractional shares at specified intervals to provide a fixed number of dollars each payment. The other specifies liquidation of an equal number of shares at each interval to provide varying payments. Since withdrawal plans are intended to be as flexible as possible in the method of payments, an investor is often allowed variations on these two basic themes.

A withdrawal plan may be adjusted to life expectancy. Suppose a retired person beginning the plan has an average expectancy of 15 years based on current mortality tables. For the first year of the plan, then, he may specify that 1/15th of the net asset value be paid to him on a monthly basis (1/180th per month). At the end of the first year, the investor refigures his life expectancy based on his higher age. He then changes his monthly payments to reflect his new longevity span, which might be about 14.3 years, to receive 1/172 per month. In each succeeding year, he adjusts the withdrawals accordingly.

The danger in such a plan, however, is that the investor will receive increasingly smaller payments each year unless the net asset value of the fund itself shows a continuing increase well in advance of its payments to him. Its advantage is that the investor will always receive an income, no matter how small.

Withdrawal rates are illustrated in the plan brochure. Usually, tables are shown of hypothetical withdrawal programs at a basic 6 per cent rate of the amount invested on varying amounts of investments.

Six per cent of the original investment, the basic rate used in most withdrawal plans, represents what most people consider an excellent rate of return. However, the percentage withdrawal does *not* truly represent "return" because it usually includes part of the principal.

Inherent Risks

Hypothetical withdrawal plans seem to show that the 6 per cent withdrawal rate has been conservative. Sizable increases in share net asset values from the mid-50's through the mid-60's have been an almost universal result. Most funds, on an average annual basis, have increased at a rate in excess of 6 per cent per annum and consequently show a greater dollar balance in fund shares *after* ten years of withdrawal than *before*.

The increase in total value of shares held is due to one significant reason: the escalation of stock values during that period. The increase in values was usually more than enough to offset the withdrawals. Thus, a plan participant who began in 1954 or 1955 and who did not take excessive withdrawals was often able to increase his principal before 1957, when the depreciation in share values for most funds *plus* the investor's payout decreased the assets per share by a dramatic ratio.

A person making an initial investment during the stock market highs in 1957 could have suffered a depreciation before the end of the year of 20 or 25 per cent or even more (plus his withdrawals). Thus, if he wished to maintain the same dollar amount of withdrawals, he would have been drawing against a smaller base and would consequently be withdrawing a larger proportion of his assets than formerly. If he was withdrawing on a percentage basis, he would be receiving a smaller amount each payment date.

Fortunately for their shareholders, most funds displayed a superior performance in 1958, recovering all or most of their losses before the year ended. If there had not been such a rapid recovery, the investor would have suffered another successive loss of capital. (Most mutual funds faced the same problem in 1962.)

During the 1950's and 1960's, business has shown the versatility necessary to overcome the setback of the business cycle. But it *is* conceivable that a series of bad years could deplete an investor's capital beyond recovery unless he took advantage of the flexibility offered by withdrawal plans and reduced the amount or rate of his payments.

Investors should look upon a withdrawal plan as a method of using capital in an orderly fashion. It should not be considered a method of permanent conservation of capital while receiving a healthy return. As in any investment, profit is not assured and there is nothing to protect the investor against possible loss in declining markets.

THE WITHDRAWAL PLAN FOLDER

The withdrawal plan folder is not a prospectus. It is considered as "sales literature" as defined in the Statement of Policy. Thus, the folder must be accompanied with, or preceded by, a fund prospectus. The points listed below are covered in the withdrawal literature published by mutual funds.

Features

Unlike voluntary and contractual accumulation plans, which are methods of periodically adding to an account, the withdrawal plan is a method of periodically subtracting from an account. It contains these advantages:

(1) **Budgeting.** This is a planned withdrawal of capital. The investor himself specifies the sum he wishes and the period between payments (limited as to the periods listed by the fund). The investor can change the method and amount of payment merely by requesting it.

If the investor wishes, he can use a regular monthly payment to support a son through college and, if he wants, may direct larger payments to handle tuition charges at certain times. He might specify that a regular sum be used for charitable contributions, perhaps for alimony, or for child support payments.

(2) **Planned Distribution.** While the man putting his son through college will, in all likelihood, want to retain at least part of the original capital, there will be others who choose to diminish their capital over a predetermined time span. Such a person might be the previously-mentioned retired individual who does not plan or wish to preserve capital for his estate. Each year he can change the amount of payment to suit his needs and life expectancy. This kind of flexibility is one of the prime features of withdrawal plans.

(3) **Capital Growth.** Under a conservative rate of withdrawal, there is a very real chance of capital growth, assuming that the fund increases in value at a rate greater than the rate of withdrawals. In this case, a small invasion of capital one year could possibly be offset by growth the following year. However, as has been pointed out, successive depreciation or a small appreciation of the asset value could well lead to a decline over the years in the amount of net assets remaining in the account.

(4) **Reporting.** All funds furnish comprehensive reports to withdrawal plan holders. Such statements, which are necessary for tax purposes, show how much was paid out in the form of ordinary income dividends, capital gains distributions, and liquidated shares. The statements are much like those given to holders of accumulation and reinvestment plans of the various funds.

(5) **Non-Forfeiture.** This is a most important provision of withdrawal plans. Just as the shares held at any time can be liquidated by the shareholder, so do the shares remaining in a withdrawal plan at his death become part of the estate.

(6) **Adding Additional Sums.** Most mutual funds require that an investor terminate any periodic investment program before a withdrawal plan can become effective. Most prospectuses have a statement to this effect:

Participants who purchase shares from the Fund during a period when shares are being redeemed from their Withdrawal Accounts to provide requested payments should realize that purchases are made at the regular offering price, which includes a sales commisison, while redemptions are made at net asset value. If an investor has an Accumulation Program, such program must be terminated before a Withdrawal Plan may take effect.

Funds will, however, permit additions to a withdrawal account. Usually they specify minimum amounts, on the order of $500 to $1,000, to be added to an original investment.

(7) **Charges and Fees.** Normally, the only charge made by the fund itself is the initial sales charge. Such charge is often less than the maximum sales charge of the fund because of the reduced charges of the larger sizes of investments needed to begin withdrawal plans. There is no sales charge, except for clerical fees, for an investor switching from an accumulation account to a withdrawal account within the same fund.

Many funds now have no charges to investors beyond the sales charge. Custodial charges on some withdrawal plans are absorbed by the underwriters.

The Table of Assumed Payments

The withdrawal plan folder may have several tables showing varying amounts of assumed initial investments, such as $10,000, $25,000 and $100,000. When optional methods of withdrawals are offered, both may be shown by illustrations of hypothetical investments.

A typical table of payments will state the period covered and the amount or the rate at which money is withdrawn. It will state that withdrawals are based on an initial net asset value—which, of course, is somewhat less than the original investment (by the amount of the sales charge).

Brochures currently in use contain statements to this effect:

(1) That the ten-year period represented was one of generally rising stock prices.

(2) That withdrawals in excess of income, especially during a period of market decline, will exhaust capital.

(3) That the results do not represent the income or capital gain or loss as of any other time period.

(4) That the tables do not adjust for any income tax for which the shareholder is liable on dividends from investment income, capital gains distributions, or on a capital gain realized from liquidation of shares.

(5) That the figures in the tables are based on the assumption that withdrawals from the fund were first taken out of income and then, if the income was insufficient to meet the planned payment, out of capital.

(6) That the amount withdrawn from investment income dividends should be regarded as income. Any difference between the investment income and the amount required to meet the withdrawal payment is to be considered as a return of capital.

The columns in each table are divided into two sections. The first is headed "Amount Withdrawn" and the second "Value of Remaining Shares."

The left-hand column under "Amount Withdrawn" is the date, which is the end of the calendar or fiscal year. The second column lists the returns to the owner from investment dividends. Over a ten-year period many funds show a gradual average increase in investment income dividends because of the growth in income from their securities. In some cases, if the income growth is large enough, the income received may eventually surpass the withdrawal amount provided that the investor withdraws at a conservative rate.

The next column to the right shows the amount which the fund found it necessary to withdraw from capital to make payments when the dividend income was insufficient to equal the specified withdrawal. Again, if the income was equal to or greater than the specified withdrawal, no payment out of capital was made to the investor. The fourth column, the total of the income dividends and withdrawal from capital, is the amount which the withdrawal plan purchaser specified for payment (or more, if dividends exceeded the specified amount). The fifth column, the cumulative total, is the year-by-year addition of total payments.

It is important to note that, for illustrative purposes, the funds must assume that *all* investment dividends, even if they exceeded the specified withdrawal amount, were paid out. In actual practice, of course, any amount beyond the specified withdrawal amount would be reinvested along with capital gains. For this reason, many funds which showed a good record of growth during the ten-year period depicted in the tables will show income dividends paid out in certain years as more than the amount specified to be withdrawn.

In practice, if the fund did so well as to show a significant increase in dividends, in all probability an investor would increase his withdrawal rate.

The second half of the table is under the overall listing of "Value of Remaining Shares." This part comprises three columns. The first "Value of Remaining Original Shares," is the liquidating value of original shares remaining after withdrawals from income and capital during the year. This amount fluctuates according to the net asset values of the shares in the fund and the share balance.

The second column, "Value of Shares Acquired through Capital Gains Distributions," is the cumulative total of such shares based on the net asset value per share.

The total of these two columns gives the last column, "Total Value of Shares Held at Year End." To the investor this is the most important column. It not only signifies the value of the remaining shares but it is a guide to future withdrawals. An increase in this column may be a signal for him to increase his withdrawals; a decrease may mean that he must reduce withdrawals if he wishes to conserve capital.

THE TAX CONSEQUENCES

Income and Capital Gains

Most ordinary income dividends, as long as they do not exceed $100 ($200 if held jointly), are currently excluded from taxable income. Such dividend income, of course, must be added to similar income from other sources in computing the exclusion.

Capital gains distributions are treated as a long-term capital gain, just as in any other mutual fund plan. Even if the shareholder received a distribution on the day after he opened a withdrawal plan, he would still be liable for this tax.

Shares which are liquidated during the course of the year present another problem. Generally, they are assumed to have been liquidated on a "FIFO", or first-in, first-out basis. Such an assumption presents no problem during liquidation of shares represented by the original investment.

But it is possible that the time will come when the initial shares have been completely liquidated. The shares next in line for liquidation are those which have been purchased through reinvestment of capital gain distributions. These shares have varying cost bases, and it could be to the shareholder's disadvantage to use FIFO, especially if the value of fund shares has shown considerable appreciation since the first capital gain reinvestments. In such a case, the planholder might be better off if he could minimize his capital gain by first liquidating the shares which have the highest cost base and thus the smallest taxable amount.

Such a method is called liquidation by *identified shares* because the shareholder is identifying or specifying the shares he is liquidating. It is important to bear in mind, however, that electing a method of liquidation must be a permanent decision. The Internal Revenue Service does not favor any changes of instruction or record keeping in this regard.

One difficulty in the matter of liquidation arises from the different manner in which the funds handle their accounts. Some funds immediately invest dividends and distributions in new shares. Thus, every check the planholder receives represents a liquidation of capital. When this is the case, the fund supplies the planholder with full particulars concerning dividends, distributions, etc. Some funds also issue to each investor an annual recapitulation for tax purposes.

Other funds hold the income dividends in a non-interest bearing escrow account until payment. Any amounts necessary to meet withdrawal payments are taken first from the escrow account and then from principal through liquidation of shares.

An investor who *transfers* previously acquired shares in a mutual fund to a withdrawal plan of that fund faces similar problems. If FIFO is used, he might face a high tax liability and would consequently be better off with a LIFO ("last-in, first -out") arrangement.

But no matter what method is used, the investor should always keep a record of transferred shares, showing the dates acquired, cost bases, and so forth.

Wash Sales

The "wash sale" rule under Section 1091 of the Internal Revenue Code is another potential problem to the investor. By reinvesting dividends and capital gains, the investor *could* be deemed to have acquired "substantially identical" securities within a 30-day period before or after the sale (liquidation) of shares required for periodic payments from the fund. If so, it is not inconceivable that any loss might be disallowed for tax purposes.

In the absence of an IRS ruling, it is not clear whether Section 1091 is applicable. However, if it is applicable, the "wash sale" disallowed losses are only temporary because the cost basis for newly acquired shares (during the 60-day period when substantially identical securities were sold) will be increased in the amount of any disallowed loss. Therefore, the subsequent sale of the "newly-acquired" shares would then give the investor either a lower capital gain or a higher capital loss because of the higher cost basis of such shares.

CONCLUSION

Although there are some tax problems to be resolved, the principle of operation of withdrawal plans is not complicated. Their convenience is enhanced by the year-end information concerning each account that is provided by most funds.

REVIEW QUESTIONS

1. What is a withdrawal plan?
2. What is the crux of any withdrawal plan?
3. What two types of basic withdrawal plans are provided by most mutual funds?
4. Discuss how a withdrawal plan may be adjusted to the life expectancy of an individual. What is the danger of such a plan?
5. Why is a withdrawal rate not really a "return".
6. For what purposes might a withdrawal plan be used?
7. When might an investor expect some capital growth from his plan?
8. Discuss the non-forfeiture provision of withdrawal plans.

9. Most mutual funds state that an investor cannot have both a withdrawal plan and an investment plan at the same time. Explain.
10. What are the advantages of the two types of withdrawal plans?
11. What are the six qualifications concerning withdrawals which are given in plan brochures?
12. As far as the investor is concerned, what is the most significant column in a withdrawal table?
13. How are capital gains distributions and dividends treated for tax purposes on the plan holder's Federal income tax return?
14. What are the disadavntages of liquidating shares on a FIFO basis?
15. Explain "liquidation by identified shares."
16. How might the investor be affected by the "wash sale" rule of the Internal Revenue Code?

Index

A

Acid test, 1-161
Accelerated depreciation, 1-163
Accounts, arbitrage, 1-193
  cash, 1-193
  commodity, 1-193
  customer, 1-193
  discretionary, 1-63, 1-194
  frozen, 1-193
  general, 1-192
  margin, 1-195
  miscellaneous "memorandum,"
    1-193
  national income and product, 1-116
  omnibus, 1-193
  payable, 1-152, 1-154
  receivable, 1-151, 1-152
  savings and loan share, 1-4, 1-5,
    1-10
  savings in banks, 1-3, 1-4, 1-10
  specialist's, 1-193
  subscription, 1-193
  supervision of (NYSE), 1-192
Accrued liabilities, 1-152, 1-154
Accumulation plans,
  mutual fund, 2-35, 2-81
Accumulation, rights of,
  mutual funds, 2-37
Accumulation units,
  variable annuity, 2-10
Acquisition or distribution,
  exchange, 1-56
Act of 1933, Securities, 1-81
Act of 1934, Securities Exchange, 1-87
Act of 1940, Investment Company, 2-53
  provisions of, 2-54
Act, Keogh (Self-employed Individuals
  Tax Retirement Act of 1962), 2-14
Act, Trust Indenture, 1-182
  Uniform Gift to Minors, 2-21
Actual market, 1-46
Administrator, registration of
  securities for, 2-25
Adjustment bond, 1-20
ADR's, 1-25
Advisers, investment, contracts, 2-58
Affiliations of directors,
  investment companies, 2-57

Agent, broker as, 1-36
  mutual fund transfer, 2-46
  registered representative as, 2-26
  transfer, 1-13, 1-43
Aggregate demand, 1-115
Agreement, underwriting, 1-32
Agreements among underwriters, 1-32
All or none order, 1-63
All or nothing,
  best efforts offering, 1-32
Alternative order, 1-63
American Depository Receipts
  (ADR's), 1-25
Amortization, depreciation
  and, 1-153, 1-163
Analysis, balance sheet, 1-157
  balance sheet, public utilities, 1-170
  corporate bonds, 1-179
  factors in individual stock, 1-174
  financial statement, 1-157
  fundamental, 1-126
  income statement, 1-161
  income statement,
    public utilities, 1-170
  industrial securities, 1-171
  market, 1-125
  market, factors in technical, 1-135
  public utilities, 1-159
  ratio, 1-158
  securities, 1-145
  securities, industry approach, 1-165
  security, 1-126
  technical, 1-125
  technical, of individual
    stocks, 1-137
Annuitant, 2-7
Annuity, concept of variable, 2-9
  fixed, 2-7
  fixed, advantages and
    disadvantages, 2-8
  non-refund, 2-8
  table, 2-8
  theory of, 2-7
Annuity, units, variable, 2-10
  variable, 2-7
Anticipation notes, bond, 1-24
  tax, 1-24, 1-108
Anticipation of death, gifts in, 2-20
Approach, fundamental or
  valuation, 1-145

INDEX

Arbitrage, 1-74
Arbitrage accounts, 1-193
Area, resistance, 1-139
Articles of incorporation, 1-13
Asked price, 1-39
Assets, 1-150, 1-152
    current, 1-108, 1-150, 1-152
    fixed, 1-152, 1-153
    total, 1-152, 1-153
Assets ratio, 1-157
Assignment and power of attorney, 1-72
Associated Press Averages, 1-131
Association, national securities, 1-99
Associations, registration of
    securities for, 2-25
Assumed bond, 1-20
At the close order, 1-63
At the opening order, 1-63
Auction, exchange bond, 1-61
Auction market, 1-29
Authority, tax, 1-184
Authorized stock, 1-17
Average, Moody, 1-131
Averages,
    Associated Press, 1-131
    Dow Jones, 1-127
    New York Herald Tribune, 1-130
    New York Times, 1-130
    stock price, 1-127
Averaging, dollar cost, 1-140

B

Balance of payments, 1-25
Balance sheet, 1-150, 1-152
Balance sheet analysis, 1-157
    public utilities, 1-170
Balance sheet, mutual fund, 2-84
Balanced fund, 2-34
Balances, customers', 1-76
Banker, investment, 1-30
    the government as, 1-110
Bank stocks, 1-172
Banks, loans by, 2-26
Bear, 1-66
Bearer bond, 1-21
Best efforts, 1-32
Best efforts, all or nothing, 1-32
Bid, 1-37
    competitive (underwriting), 1-33
    firm, 1-45
    special, NYSE, 1-57
Bid price, 1-39
Bid wanted, 1-45
Bill, Treasury, 1-6, 1-22
Blanket mortgage, 1-20

Block procedures, NYSE, 1-54
Block purchase or sale,
    specialist, NYSE, 1-55
Blue sky laws, 1-97
Board, Federal Reserve, 1-111
Bond analysis, 1-179
Bond and preferred stock fund, 2-34
Bond anticipation note, 1-24
Bond auction, exchange, 1-61
Bond conversion privileges, 1-181
Bond fund, 2-33
Bond house, 1-37
Bond interest rate, 1-181
Bond marketability, 1-181
Bond, municipal, ratios, 1-185
Bond, municipal, tax status, 1-185
Bond quotations, 1-42, 1-61
Bond ratings, 1-181
Bonds, types of:, 1-19
    adjustment, 1-20
    assumed, 1-20
    bearer, 1-21
    cabinet, 1-61
    callable, 1-21, 1-182
    closed-end mortgage, 1-20
    collateral trust, 1-20
    consolidated mortgage, 1-20
    convertible, 1-21
    corporate, 1-4, 1-7, 1-10, 1-179
    coupon, 1-21
    debenture, 1-20
    divisional, 1-19
    E & H, 1-3, 1-4, 1-10
    first lien, 1-19
    first mortgage, 1-19
    free, 1-61
    fully registered, 1-21
    general mortgage, 1-20
    general obligation, 1-23
    guaranteed, 1-20
    income, 1-20, 1-183
    joint, 1-19
    junior mortgage, 1-19
    limited obligation, 1-23
    limited open-end mortgage, 1-21
    limited tax, 1-23
    long-term, 1-19
    medium-term, 1-19
    mortgage, 1-19
    municipal, 1-4, 1-6, 1-10, 1-23, 1-184
    non-callable, 1-21
    open-end mortgage, 1-20
    participating, 1-20
    prior lien, 1-19
    refunding, 1-21
    registered, 1-21

Bonds, types of: (continued)
    revenue, 1-20
    savings, 1-22
    secured, 1-19
    senior mortgage, 1-19
    serial, 1-21
    series, 1-21
    sinking fund, 1-21
    short-term, 1-19
    split coupon, 1-20
    surety, 1-72
    Treasury, 1-4, 1-6, 1-10, 1-22
    unlimited tax, 1-23
Bond yield, 1-147
Bonding requirements,
    management company, 2-59
Book, specialist's, 1-51
Book value, 1-47, 1-153
Book value per share ratio, 1-157
Branch manager, NYSE,
    qualifications for, 1-191
Branch office, NASD, 1-189
Breadth index, 1-135
Breadth of the market, 1-135
Break-point sales, mutual fund, 2-73
Broker, 1-36, 1-89
    as agent, 1-36
    commission, 1-52
    dealer registration, 1-37
    independent floor, 1-52
    two-dollar, 1-52
Brokers and dealers, 1-36
Brokers loans, 1-110
Brokers, loans by, 2-26
Building and loan (see "Savings and
    loan.")
Bulk segregation of securities, 1-76
Bull, 1-66
Business cycle, 1-114, 1-121
Buyer's option (NASD), 1-43
Buying in, NASD, 1-44
    NYSE, 1-73
By-laws, corporation, 1-13

C

Cabinet bonds, 1-61
Call (option), 1-68
Callable bond, 1-21
Callable preferred stock, 1-17
Callable provisions of bond, 1-182
Capital, money and, 1-106
    owner's, 1-155
    stability of, as mutual fund
        objective, 2-32
    working, 1-158

Capital gains, holding period, 2-17
    how taxed, 2-16
    mutual fund, 2-36
    losses, 2-17
Capital market, 1-108
    secondary, 1-109
    markets, money and, 1-107
Capital shares, leveraged fund, 2-6
Capital stock, 1-16
Capital structure, 1-155, 1-158
Capital surplus, 1-152, 1-155
Capitalization, 1-155
Carryover loss, 2-17
Cash accounts, customer, 1-193
Cash as a speculation, 1-3
Cash delivery, NASD, 1-42
    NYSE, 1-70
Cash holdings, 1-161
Cash on hand and in banks, 1-151, 1-152
Cash, speculation in, 1-3
Cash trade, 1-46
Cash values, life insurance, 1-4, 1-5, 1-10
Cash values of life insurance
    (on balance sheet), 1-152
Cash reserves, life insurance, 1-5, 1-10
Cash surrender values, 1-4, 1-5, 1-10
Certificate,
    equipment trust, 1-22
    face amount, 2-56
    receivers', 1-22
    stock, 1-13
    voting trust, 1-18
Certificate of incorporation, 1-13
Certificates of indebtedness, 1-22
Changes,
    economic, 1-118
    short-term economic, 1-121
Changes in margin requirements, 1-113
    net assets, mutual fund, 2-88
    policy, investment company, 2-58
    share value, mutual fund, 2-74
Charge, sales, mutual fund, 2-36, 2-43
Charges,
    interest, 1-156, 1-157
    prepaid, 1-152, 1-153
Chart reading, 1-138
Charter, corporate, 1-13
Charts,
    line, 1-138
    point and figure, 1-138
Circular, offering, 1-34
Classes of corporate securities, 1-15
Classification of mutual funds
    by management, 2-34
    by objective, 2-32
    by portfolio, 2-33
Clearing Corporation, Stock, 1-71

Clearing stock, over-the-counter, 1-44
Closed-end investment
 company, 1-9, 2-56
 mortgage bond, 1-20
Collateral trust bond, 1-20
Commercial credit, 1-107
Commercial paper, 1-108
Commission broker, 1-52
Commissions,
 stock exchange, 1-64
 underwriting, 1-31
Commodities as a speculation, 1-3
Commodity accounts, customer, 1-193
Commodity futures, 1-3
 markets, 1-109
Common stock, 1-16
 dividends on, 1-14
Common stock fund, 2-34
 ratio, 1-158
Common, tenants in, 2-24
Company, mutual
 fund management, 2-44
Comparisons, mutual fund, 2-105, 2-112
Competitive bidding, underwriting, 1-33
Completion of contractual plan, 2-124
Computation of offering price,
 mutual fund, 2-72, 2-86
Computation of margin, 1-196
Concentration of sales
 (in analysis), 1-161
Concession, dealer, mutual fund, 2-43
Confirmation, 1-134
Conservation of principal as a
 mutual fund objective, 2-32
Consolidated mortgage bond, 1-20
Consolidations, 1-176
Constant divisor, stock average, 1-127
Constant dollar formula, 1-141
Constant ratio formula, 1-142
Constructive receipt
 (for tax purposes), 2-38
Contingencies, reserves for, 1-162
Contingent interest, coverage of,
 railroads, 1-167
 liabilities, 1-154
 order, 1-64
Cooperative, mutual fund not a, 2-108
Consumer financing, 1-109
 price index, 1-117
Contract, investment, 1-81
 investment advisers and
  underwriting, 2-58
Contractual plan, 2-62, 2-115
 custodian, 2-128
 prospectus, 2-120
 rights and privileges, 2-123

Contractual plan,
 tax status of, 2-127
 when completed and when
  terminated, 2-124
Conversion privileges, bond, 1-181
Convertible bonds, 1-21
 preferred stock, 1-17
Corner, 1-92
Corporate bonds, 1-4, 1-7, 1-10
 securities, classes of 1-11, 1-15
 senior securities, 1-179
 stock, 1-4, 1-8, 1-10, 1-13, 1-15, 1-16
 stock ownership, 1-13
 taxes, 2-18
Corporation, 1-11
 by-laws, 1-13
 charter, 1-13
 domestic, 1-12
 foreign, 1-12
 formation of, 1-12
 personal, 1-7
Corporation,
 registration of securities for, 2-25
 Stock Clearing, 1-71
Cost averaging, dollar, 1-140
Cost base, exchange-type funds, 2-49
Cost of goods sold, 1-156
Cost or market, 1-151
Coupon bond, 1-21
Coverage of contingent interest,
 railroads, 1-167
 fixed charges, railroads, 1-167
 preferred dividends,
  railroads, 1-167
 senior charges, 1-159
 senior charges ratio, 1-158
Credit,
 basis for money and, 1-106
 commercial, 1-107
 investment, 1-107
 regulation of, 1-112, 2-26
Cumulative preferred stock, 1-16
 voting, 1-15
Current assets, 1-108, 1-150, 1-152
 liabilities, 1-108, 1-152, 1-154
 maturity of long-term
  debt, 1-152, 1-154
 ratio, 1-160
Custodian,
 contractual plan, 2-128
 mutual fund, 2-45
 mutual fund, function of, 2-103
Custodian fee, 2-56
 qualifications, 2-59
Customer accounts, 1-192
 and the registered
  representative, 2-25
 market, 1-108

Customer's credit balance, 1-76
    debit balance, 1-76
    equity, 1-76, 1-195
Customers' balances, 1-76
    securities, 1-75
Cyclical changes, 1-118

D

Daily fluctuations, 1-134
Date,
    ex-dividend, 1-46
    record, 1-46
    settlement, 1-46
    trade, 1-46
Day order, 1-62
Dealer, odd-lot, 1-52
Dealer as a principal, 1-37
Dealer concession, mutual fund, 2-43
Dealers and brokers, 1-36
Death, gifts in anticipation of, 2-20
Debenture (bond), 1-20
Debit balance, customer's, 1-76
Debt,
    evidence of, 1-1
    Federal, 1-185
    floating, 1-24
    overlapping, 1-24
    per capita, 1-185
Debt to property ratio,
    municipal bonds, 1-185
Debt-equity ratio, 1-159
Deceptive devices, 1-91
Deed of trust, 1-19
Defensive issues, 1-175
Deflation, inflation and, 1-119
Deflation hedge, 2-4
Delayed delivery,
    NASD, 1-42
    regular way, NYSE, 1-70
Deliveries,
    NASD, 1-42
    NYSE, 1-70
Delivery,
    cash, NASD, 1-42
    cash, NYSE, 1-70
    delayed, NASD, 1-42
    delayed regular way, NYSE, 1-70
    good, 1-43, 1-47
    regular way, NASD, 1-42
    regular way, NYSE, 1-70
    seller's option, NASD, 1-43
    seller's option, NYSE, 1-70
Demand deposits, 1-107
Denial of registration, grounds for, 1-93
Depletion or exhaustion, 1-163

Deposits, demand, 1-107
Depreciation, 1-152, 1-156
Depreciation and
    amortization, 1-156, 1-163
Differential, odd-lot, 1-64
Directorate, interlocking, 2-44
Directors,
    investment companies,
        affiliations of, 2-57
    mutual fund, 2-41
Discount,
    at a, 2-6
    bond at a, 1-147
    underwriting, 1-31
Discounting the future, 1-146
Discretionary accounts, 1-63, 1-94
Discretionary order, 1-63
Disposable personal income, 1-116
Disregard tape order, 1-63
Distribution or acquisition,
    exchange, 1-56
Distribution,
    primary, 1-30
    secondary, 1-30, 1-59
Distributions, mutual fund,
    presentation of, 2-98
Distributor, mutual fund, 2-45
Districts, tax, 1-184
Diversified investment
    company, 2-56, 2-70
Dividend, 1-14, 1-146
    common and preferred stock, 1-14
    ex-, 1-40, 1-46
    income, mutual fund, 2-36
    property, 1-147
    savings and loan account, 1-5
    stock, 1-147
Dividend on, 1-46
Dividend payout ratio, 1-159
Dividend reinvestment plan,
    mutual fund, 2-35, 2-80
Dividends payable, 1-152, 1-154
Divisional bond, 1-19
Dollar-cost-averaging, 1-140, 2-109
Domestic corporation, 1-12
Do not reduce order, 1-63
Dow Jones averages, 1-127
Dow theory, 1-132
Dual fund (leveraged fund), 2-6
Due diligence meeting, 1-35

E

E & H bonds, 1-22
Earned surplus, 1-152, 1-155
Earning power, 1-174

Earnings, retained, 1-155
Earnings, securities analysis of, 1-145
Earnings per share of common,
    railroads, 1-167
Earnings ratio, 1-158
Economic changes, 1-118
    growth, 1-118
    indicators, 1-115
    policy, international, 1-122
    trends, 1-106, 1-114
    trends and the business cycle, 1-114
Effective sale, round lot, 1-64
Either/or order, 1-63
Emergency Fund, 2-2, 2-3
Employer as a principal, 2-26
Entirety, tenants by the, 2-21
Equalization factor, 2-88
Equalization tax, interest, 1-24
Equipment trust certificate, 1-22
Equity,
    customer's 1-76, 1-195
    stockholders', 1-152, 1-153, 1-155
Equity funding, 1-81
Equity security, 1-89
Estate and inheritance taxes, 2-19
Evidence of debt, 1-1
    of ownership, 1-1
Exchange, definition of, 1-88
Exchange bond auction, 1-61
Exchange distribution or
    acquisition, 1-56
Exchange member, 1-89
Exchange-type funds, 2-47
    cost base, 2-49
    exchange procedure, 2-48
    redemptions and taxes, 2-50
Exchanges, stock, 1-49
Ex-dividend, 1-40, 1-46
Ex-dividend date, 1-46
Executor,
    registration of securities for, 2-25
Exempt securities, 1-194
Exempted securities, 1-82
Exempted transactions, 1-82
Exemption, Regulation A, 1-34
Exhaustion, depletion or, 1-163
Expense ratio,
    insurance companies, 1-173
Expense,
    selling and administrative, 1-156
Export-Import Bank, 1-123

F

Face-amount certificate, 2-56
Factors in individual stock
    analysis, 1-174

Factors in market analysis,
    technical, 1-135
Features of principal types of
    investments, 1-10
Federal debt, 1-185
Federal registration, mutual fund, 2-103
Federal Reserve Board, 1-111
Fee, custodian, 2-46
Fee, mutual fund management, 2-44
Fee, mutual fund underwriter's, 2-43
Fiduciaries and mutual funds, 2-109
FIFO, 1-151
Fill or kill order, 1-62
Financial information, sources of, 1-148
Financial news ticker, 1-149
Financial planning, 2-1
Financial position,
    public utilities, 1-171
    railroads, 1-168
Financial ratios, 1-157
Financial ratios in railroad
    analysis, 1-167
Financial statement analysis, 1-157
Financial statements, 1-150
    mutual fund, 2-82
Financing, consumer, 1-109
Firm bid, 1-45
Firm offer, 1-46
First in, first out, 1-151
First lien bond, 1-19
First mortgage bond, 1-19
Fiscal management, 1-111
Fiscal year, 1-150
Fixed annuity, 2-7
Fixed annuities,
    advantages and disadvantages, 2-8
Fixed assets, 1-152, 1-153
Fixed assets to net worth ratio, 1-160
Fixed charges,
    municipal, 1-185
    railroads, coverage of, 1-167
    ratio of earnings to, 1-180
Flat, traded, 1-46
Floating debt, 1-24
Floor broker, independent, 1-52
Floor members, exchange, 1-52
Floor trader, 1-52
Foreign corporation, 1-12
Foreign exchange market, 1-109
Foreign securities, 1-24
Formation of corporations, 1-12
Forms of investment, 1-3
Forms of speculation, 1-2
Formula investing, 1-139
    constant dollar, 1-141
    constant ratio, 1-142

Formula Investing—(Continued)
 dollar cost averaging, 1-140
 variable ratio, 1-143
Fraudulent transactions, 1-85
Free bonds, 1-61
Front-end load plan, 2-115
Frozen accounts, 1-193
Full registration, NYSE, 1-191
Fully managed type mutual funds, 2-35
Fully registered bond, 1-21
Function of custodian,
 mutual fund, 2-103
Fundamental analysis, 1-126
Fundamental approach, 1-145
Fund (see Mutual Fund for open-end
 investment companies)
Fund,
 dual, 2-6
 emergency, 2-2, 2-3
 leveraged, 2-6
Funds, exchange-type, 2-47
Fungible securities, 1-76
Future, discounting the, 1-146
Future interest, gift of, 2-20
Futures, commodity, 1-3

G

Gambling, 1-2
General accounts, customer, 1-192
General mortgage bond, 1-20
General obligation, 1-23
General qualifications for
 NYSE listing, 1-77
Geographical sales, 1-161
Gift of future or present interest, 2-20
Gift taxes, 2-20
Gifts in anticipation of death, 2-20
Gifts to minors, 2-21
Gifts to Minors Act, Uniform, 2-21
Give-ups, NYSE, 1-73
GNP (Gross National Product), 1-116
Good delivery, 1-43, 1-47
Good 'til cancelled order, 1-62
Government as a banker, 1-110
Government E & H bonds, 1-3, 1-4, 1-10
 (for other Government bonds,
 see Treasury)
Government paper, 1-22
Government securities, 1-151, 1-183
Government spending, 1-120
Gross National Product (GNP), 1-116
Grounds for denial of registration, 1-93
Group purchase, 1-32
Group selling, 1-32
Group underwriting, 1-32

Growth as a fund objective, 2-33
Growth ratios, 1-159
Growth stock, 1-159, 1-175
GTC order, 1-62
Guarantee of signature, 1-44
Guaranteed bond, 1-20
Guaranteed securities, 1-183
Guaranteed stock, 1-17
Guardian, registration of
 securities for, 2-24

H

H bonds, 1-3, 1-4, 1-10
Hedges, inflation and deflation, 2-4
Highs and lows, new, 1-137
High-priced stocks, movement of, 1-136
History of investments companies, 2-30
Holding period for capital gains, 2-17
Holdings, cash, 1-161

I

Immediate or cancel order, 1-62
Improved property, 1-7
Income,
 disposable personal, 1-116
 national, 1-116
 other (as income statement
  item), 1-157
Income and products account,
 national, 1-116
Income as a mutual fund objective, 2-33
Income bond, 1-20, 1-183
Income dividends, mutual fund, 2-36
Income plan, mutual fund, 2-80
Income shares, leveraged
 (dual) fund, 2-6
Income statement, 1-150, 1-155, 1-156
Income statement analysis, 1-161
 public utilities, 1-170
 railroads, 1-166
Income stock, 1-175
Income taxes, 2-15
Indebtedness, certificate of, 1-22
Indenture Act, Trust, 1-182
Indenture of trust, 1-19
Independent floor broker, 1-52
Index,
 consumer price, 1-117
 industrial production, 1-117
 Merrill Lynch, 1-132
 NYSE common stock, 1-132
 SEC, 1-132

Index— (Continued)
Standard & Poor's, 1-131
stock, 1-126
Indexes,
breadth, 1-135
stock price, 1-131
Indication of interest, 1-35
Indicators, economic, 1-115
Individuals, registration of
securities for, 2-22
Industrial averages, 1-135
Industrial production, index of, 1-11.
Industrial securities, 1-171
Industry approach, 1-167
Industry fund, 2-34
Inflation and deflation, 1-119
Inflation hedge, 2-4
Information, sources of financial, 1-148
Inheritance and estate taxes, 2-19
Initial margin, 1-65, 1-198
Inspection, stockholder's right of, 1-15
Insurance, purpose of life, 2-2
Insurance cash reserves, 1-5
Insurance cash values, 1-4, 1-5, 1-10
Insurance companies, analysis of, 1-173
Intangible property taxes, 2-18
Intent, mutual fund letter of, 2-37
Interdealer quotations, 1-39
Interest, gift of future or present, 2-20
Interest, indication of interest, 1-35
Interest charges, 1-156, 1-157
Interest equalization tax, 1-24
Interest rate, bond, 1-181
Interlocking directorate, 2-44
International Bank for Reconstruction
and Development, 1-121
International economic policy, 1-22
International Monetary Fund, 1-121
Inter-vivos trust, registration of
securities for, 2-24
Intestate, 2-19
Inventories, 1-151, 1-162
Inventory turnover ratio, 1-160
Inventorying a stock, 1-37
Investing, formula, 1-139
Investment,
ownership, 1-4
types of, 1-3
Investment and speculation, 1-1
Investment advisers' contracts, 2-58
Investment banker, 1-30
Investment in other people's debts, 1-3
Investment companies
(see also Mutual Funds), 1-173
Investment companies,
affiliations of directors, 2-57
analysis of, 1-173

closed-end, 1-9, 1-10
history of, 2-30
leveraged (dual), 2-6
open-end, 1-8, 1-10
short sales by, 2-58
Investment companies as
investments, 1-4, 1-8, 1-10
Investment companies in financial
planning, 2-5
Investment company,
closed-end, 1-9, 1-10
diversified, 2-70
loans by, 2-60
open-end, 1-8, 1-10
regulated, 2-37
small business, 1-8
Investment Company Act
of 1940, 1-97, 2-53
Investment Company Act,
provisions of, 2-54
Investment company defined, 2-55
Investment company management,
prospectus information, 2-78
Investment company periodic
reports, 2-62
policies and restrictions, 2-71
policy changes, 2-58
principal underwriter, 2-78
prospectus, 2-67
quotations, 1-41
shares, liquidating value, 2-77
shares, redemption or
repurchase, 2-77
size, 2-58
underwriting contracts, 2-58
Investment contract, 1-81
Investment credit, 1-107
Investment trusts, real estate, 1-6, 2-11
Investments,
features of principal types of, 1-10
schedule of (portfolio), 2-83
Investments in financial planning, 2-4
Issue, new, 1-30
Issuer, 1-32, 1-89
Issues, defensive, 1-175

J

Joint bond, 1-19
registrants, 2-22
tenants with right of
survivorship, 2-22
venture, 1-8
Junior mortgage bond, 1-19
Jurisdiction, Office of Supervisory,
NASD, 1-189

K

Keogh Act, 2-14

L

Large block procedures, NYSE, 1-54
Last in, first out, 1-151
Law,
    unauthorized practice of, 2-26
    model, 2-21
Laws, Blue Sky, 1-80, 1-97
Legal list, 1-98
Lending to member banks, 1-112
Letter of intent, mutual fund, 2-37
Level, support, 1-139
Leverage, 1-178
Leveraged (dual) fund, 2-6
Liabilities, 1-152, 1-154
    accrued, 1-152, 1-154
    contingent, 1-154
    current, 1-108, 1-152, 1-154
Liability,
    limited, 1-13
    mutual fund shareholder's tax, 2-38
    stockholder personal, 1-13
Life insurance,
    adequacy of, 2-3
    purpose of, 2-2
Life insurance cash
    values, 1-4, 1-5, 1-10, 1-152, 1-153
Life insurance reserves, 1-5
LIFO, 1-151
Limit on sales charge, mutual fund, 2-78
Limit order, 1-62
Limited liability, 1-13
    obligation, 1-23
    open-end mortgage bond, 1-21
    partner, 1-8
    registration, NYSE, 1-191
    tax bond, 1-23
Line charts, 1-138
Liquidating value,
    mutual fund shares, 2-77
Liquidation rights, stockholder's, 1-14
Liquidity, 1-158
List, legal, 1-98
Listed security, 1-42
Listing standards,
    NYSE, 1-77
    other exchanges, 1-78
Loans, brokers', 1-110
Loans by banks, 2-26
Loans by brokers, 2-26
Loans by investment companies, 2-60

Long-term bonds, 1-19
    changes, 1-118
    debt, 1-152, 1-155
    debt, current
        maturity of, 1-152, 1-154
Loss carryover, 2-17
Loss ratio, insurance company, 1-173
Losses, capital, 2-17
Low-priced stocks, movement of, 1-136

M

Maintaining the offering price,
    mutual funds, 2-61
Maintenance margin, 1-65, 1-198
    ratio, railroads, 1-167
Maloney Act, 1-99
Management,
    classification of mutual
        funds by, 2-34
    fiscal, 1-111
    mutual fund, 2-42
    mutual fund, measure of
        success, 2-32
    mutual fund, prospectus
        information, 2-78
Management companies defined, 2-56
Management company,
    mutual fund, 2-44
Management company bonding
    requirements, 2-59
Management fees, mutual fund, 2-44
Manager, syndicate, 1-32
Managerial performance,
    measures of, 1-159
Managing underwriter, 1-32
Manipulation, 1-90, 1-94
Margin, 1-65, 1-195
Margin,
    computing, 1-196
    initial and maintenance, 1-65, 1-198
Margin accounts, 1-195
    requirements, 1-198
Margin requirements, changes in, 1-113
Market,
    actual, 1-46
    auction, 1-29
    breadth of the, 1-135
Market,
    capital, 1-108
    commodity, 1-109
    customer, 1-108
    foreign exchange, 1-109
    money, 1-108
    money and capital, 1-107
    negotiated, 1-29

Market—(Continued)
 organized, 1-108
 over-the-counter, 1-29
 secondary capital, 1-109
 stock exchanges, 1-29
 subject, 1-46
 third, 1-29
 workout, 1-46
Market analysis, 1-125
 technical factors in, 1-135
Market order,
 NASD, 1-46
 NYSE, 1-62
Market position, 1-146
Market reaction to news, 1-137
Market seasonal movements, 1-137
Market value, 1-47
Market volume, 1-49, 1-136
Marketability, bond, 1-181
Markets, types of, 1-29
Marking to the market,
 NASD, 1-44
 NYSE, 1-73
Mark-up, 1-31
Material out of context, 2-112
Maturity, current,
 of long-term debt, 1-152, 1-154
 yield to, 1-148
Measure of success,
 mutual fund management, 2-32
Measures of managerial
 performance, 1-159
Medium-term bond, 1-19
Meeting, due diligence, 1-35
Member, exchange, 1-89
Member banks, lending to, 1-112
Memorandum accounts,
 miscellaneous, 1-193
Mergers, 1-176
Merrill Lynch index, 1-132
Minors, gifts to, 2-21
Minors Act, Uniform Gift to, 2-21
MIP (monthly investment plan),
 NYSE, 2-12
Miscellaneous "memorandum"
 accounts, 1-193
Misrepresenting return on
 mutual funds, 2-100
Model Law, 2-21
Monetary policy, 1-111
Money and capital, 1-106
Money and capital markets, 1-107
Money and credit, basis for, 1-106
Money system, 1-106
Monthly investment plan of
 NYSE (MIP), 2-12
Moody averages, 1-131

Moral suasion, Federal Reserve
 Board, 1-113
Mortgage, 1-4, 1-6, 1-10
Mortgage, blanket, 1-20
Mortgage bond, 1-19
Movements,
 low- and high-priced stocks, 1-136
 seasonal, 1-137
Multiplier, stock average, 1-127
Municipal bond, 1-4, 1-6, 1-10, 1-23, 1-184
Municipal bond, tax status of, 1-185
Municipal bond ratios, 1-185
Municipal fixed charges, 1-185
Municipalities, 1-184
Mutual fund(s):, 1-8, 2-29
 accumulation plans, 2-35, 2-81
 and taxes, 2-37
 as a trust, 2-46
 balance sheet, 2-84
 balanced, 2-34
 bond, 2-33
Mutual fund(s):
 bond and preferred stock, 2-34
 break-point sales, 2-73
 capital gains, 2-36
 changes in net assets, 2-88
 changes in share value, 2-74
 classification of by
  management, 2-34
 classification of by objective, 2-32
 classification of by portfolio, 2-33
 common stock, 2-34
 comparisons, 2-105, 2-112
 custodian, 2-45
 custodian, function of, 2-103
 dealer concession, 2-43
 directors, 2-41
 distributor, 2-45
 dividend reinvestment
  plan, 2-35, 2-80
 Federal registration of, 2-103
 fully managed type, 2-35
 income dividends, 2-36
 income plan, 2-80
 industry, 2-34
 in financial planning, 2-5
Mutual fund(s):
 letter of intent, 2-37
 liquidating value, 2-77
 maintaining the offering price, 2-61
 management, 2-42
 management,
  prospectus information, 2-78
 management company, 2-44
 management fees, 2-44
 misrepresenting return, 2-100
 net asset value, 2-43

Mutual fund(s)—(Continued)
    new capital to industry, 2-107
    not a cooperative, 2-108
    objectives, 2-32
    offering price, 2-43
    officers, 2-42
    open account, 2-81
    organization of, 2-41
    percentage return, 2-97
    performance charts
        and tables, 2-108
    personnel, 2-41
    placement of orders by, 2-46
    policies and restrictions, 2-71
    portfolio, 2-83
    presentation of distributions, 2-98
    preservation or **gain**
        of capital, 2-102
    price make-up sheet, 2-85
    principal underwriter, 2-78
    prospectus, 2-67
    purchase of shares, 2-35
    quotations, 1-41
    rate of return, 2-96
    regulated, 2-37
    restricted management type, 2-34
    rights of accumulation, 2-37
    sales charge, 2-36, 2-40
    sales charge literature
        requirement, 2-111
    sales literature, 2-94
    selection by fiduciaries, 2-109
    shareholders, 2-41
    shareholders' tax liability, 2-38
    shares, redemption or
        repurchase, 2-77
    shares, value at redemption, 2-104
    statement of income and
        expense, 2-87
    switching, 2-111
    systematic investing plan, 2-81
    transfer agent, 2-46
    underwriter, 2-45
    underwriter's fee, 2-43
    use of published material on, 2-112
    voluntary plan, 2-81
    withdrawal plan, 2-35, 2-82, 2-133

N

Name, street, 1-75
NASD (National Association of
    Securities Dealers, Inc.), 1-99, 1-187
    branch office, 1-189
    history of, 1-100
    Office of Supervisory
        Jurisdiction, 1-189
    purposes of, 1-104
    registration of principals, 1-189
    requirements for registered
        representatives, 1-187
    supervision of registered
        representatives, 1-189
National income, 1-116
National income and products
    accounts, 1-116
National securities association, 1-99
Negotiated market, 1-29
Negotiated underwriting, 1-33
Net asset value per share,
    mutual fund, 2-43
Net national product, 1-116
Net operating earnings, 1-172
Net price, underwriting, 1-36
Net profits, 1-172
Net quick assets to current liabilities
    ratio, 1-160
Net worth, 1-153
New capital to industry,
    mutual funds, 2-107
New highs and lows, 1-137
New issue, 1-2, 1-30
News, market reaction to, 1-137
New York Herald Tribune
    averages, 1-130
New York Stock Exchange
    (NYSE):, 1-49
    arbitrage, 1-74
    as an auction market, 1-50
    background and history, 1-49
    buying in, 1-73
    commission broker, 1-52
    commissions, 1-64
    common stock index, 1-132
    current operating procedures, 1-51
    customers' balances, 1-76
    customers' securities, 1-75
    deliveries, 1-70
    exchange bond auction, 1-61
    exchange distribution or
        acquisition, 1-56
    floor members, 1-52
    general qualifications for
        listing, 1-77
    give-ups, 1-73
    how governed, 1-50
    independent floor broker, 1-52
    large block procedures, 1-54
    listing standards, 1-77
New York Stock Exchange (NYSE):
    margins, 1-65

New York Stock Exchange (NYSE)—
    (Continued)
    market and limit order, 1-62
    marking to the market, 1-73
    monthly investment plan
        (MIP), 2-12
    newspaper quotations, 1-59
    odd-lot orders, 1-64
    odd lots, 1-52
    qualifications for branch
        manager, 1-191
    registered representative,
    definition of, 1-190
    registered representative,
    supervision of, 1-191
    registration, types of, 1-191
    round lot unit of trading, 1-52
    secondary distribution, 1-59
    security options, 1-67
    short selling, 1-66
    special offering or bid, 1-57
    specialist, 1-51
    specialist block purchase
        or sale, 1-55
    Stock Clearing Corporation, 1-71
    stock rights, 1-69
    stock transfer, 1-71
    trading post, 1-53
    typical transaction, 1-52
    when-issued securities, 1-73
New York Times averages, 1-130
Newspaper quotations, 1-39, 1-59
    bond, 1-61
    Government Agency, 1-41
    mutual funds, 1-41
    over-the-counter market, 1-40
    stock exchange, 1-60
Non-callable bond, 1-21
Non-cumulative preferred stock, 1-16
Non-cumulative voting, 1-15
Non-diversified investment
    company, 2-56
Non-recurring items, 1-162
Non-refund annuity, 2-8
Not held order, 1-63
Note payable, 1-152, 1-154
Note receivable, 1-151, 1-152
Notes,
    bond anticipation, 1-24
    tax anticipation, 1-24, 1-108
    Treasury, 1-6, 1-22

O

Objective, classification of mutual
    funds by, 2-32
Objectives of mutual funds, 2-32

Obligations,
    general, 1-23
    limited, 1-23
    state, 1-23
    Treasury, 1-183
Obsolescence, 1-153
Odd lot, 1-52, 1-64
Odd-lot behavior, 1-136
    dealer, 1-52
    differential, 1-64
    orders, 1-64
Offer, 1-37
Offer, firm, 1-46
Offering,
    private, 1-34
    special, NYSE, 1-57
Offering circular, 1-34
    price, computation of, 2-72, 2-86
    price, mutual fund, 2-43
    price, maintenance of, 2-61
    wanted, 1-45
Office, branch, NASD, 1-189
Office of Supervisory Jurisdiction,
    NASD, 1-189
Officers, mutual fund, 2-41
Omnibus accounts, 1-193
Open account, mutual fund, 2-81
Open-end investment
    company, 1-8, 1-10, 2-56
Open-end mortgage bond, 1-20
Open-end mortgage bond, limited, 1-21
Open market operations, 1-113
Open order, 1-46, 1-62
Operating profit, 1-156
Operating profit ratios,
    public utilities, 1-171
Operating ratios, railroads, 1-167
Operations, open market, 1-113
Option,
    buyer's, 1-43
    call, 1-68
    protective use of, 1-69
    put, 1-68
    security, 1-67
    seller's, 1-43
    speculative use of, 1-68
Order(s):
    all or none, 1-63
    alternative, 1-63
    at the close, 1-63
    at the opening, 1-63
    cancel, 1-62
Order(s):
    contingent, 1-64
    day, 1-62
    discretionary, 1-63
    disregard tape, 1-63

Order(s)—(Continued)
    do not reduce (DNR), 1-63
    fill or kill, 1-62
    good 'til cancelled (GTC), 1-62
    immediate or cancel, 1-62
    limit, 1-62
    market, 1-46, 1-62
    not held, 1-63
    odd-lot, 1-64
    open, 1-46, 1-62
    percentage, 1-63
    scale, 1-64
    stop, 1-62
    stop limit, 1-62
    switch, 1-64
    take time, 1-63
    time, 1-64
Orders by mutual funds,
    placement of, 2-46
Organization of mutual funds, 2-41
Organized market, 1-108
Other people's debts, 1-4
Out of context material, 2-112
Outright purchase of mutual fund
    shares, 2-35
Outstanding stock, 1-18
Over-the-counter (OTC) market, 1-29
    functions of, 1-30
    quotations, 1-40
Overlapping debt, 1-24
Ownership,
    evidence of, 1-1
    investment in, 1-4
Owners' capital, 1-155

P

Paper,
    commercial, 1-108
    prime, 1-4
Par value, 1-147
Partially unsecured, 1-44
Participating bond, 1-20
Participating preferred stock, 1-16
Partner,
    limited, 1-8
    silent, 1-8
Partnership, 1-4, 1-8, 1-10
    registration of securities for, 2-25
Payable,
    accounts, 1-152, 1-154
    dividends, 1-152, 1-154
    note, 1-152, 1-154
    taxes, 1-152, 1-154
Payments, balance of, 1-25
Penalty plan, 2-115

Pension or profit-sharing trusts,
    registration of securities for, 2-25
Per capita debt, 1-185
Percentage approaches, 1-193
Percentage order, 1-63
Percentage return, mutual fund,
    charts and tables, 2-108
Periodic payment plan, 2-62
Personal corporations, 1-7
Personal income, disposable, 1-116
Personal liability of stockholder, 1-13
Personalty, 1-3
Personnel, mutual fund, 2-41
Physical data, use of in analysis, 1-161
Physical reserves, 1-161
Pink sheets, 1-37
Placement, private, 1-33
Placement of orders by
    mutual funds, 2-46
Plan:
    accumulation, mutual fund, 2-35
    contractual, 2-62, 2-115
    dividend reinvestment,
        mutual fund, 2-35
    front-end load, 2-115
    Keogh, 2-14
    mutual fund withdrawal, 2-113, 2-35
    penalty, 2-115
    periodic payment, 2-62, 2-115
    prepaid charge, 2-115
    self-employed individuals'
        retirement, 2-14
Plan prospectus, contractual, 2-120
Planning, financial, 2-1
Point and figure charts, 1-138
Policies and restrictions,
    mutual fund, 2-71
Policy,
    international economic, 1-122
    monetary, 1-111
    Statement of, SEC, 2-93
Policy changes, investment
    company, 2-58
Pool, 1-92
Population trends, 1-120
Portfolio,
    classification of mutual
        funds by, 2-33
    mutual fund, 2-83
Position,
    market, 1-146
    security, 1-37
Post, trading, 1-51, 1-53
Pre-emptive rights, 1-15
Preferred dividends, coverage of,
    railroads, 1-167
Preferred stock, 1-16

Preferred stock,
    analysis of, 1-182
    callable, 1-17
    convertible, 1-17
    cumulative, 1-16
    dividends on, 1-14
    non-cumulative, 1-16
    participating, 1-16
    prior, 1-16
Premium, 1-148
Premium, at a, 2-6
Prepaid charge plan, 2-115
Prepaid charges, 1-152, 1-153
Present interest, gift of, 2-20
Presentation of mutual fund
    distributions, 2-98
Preservation or gain of capital,
    mutual funds, 2-102
Price,
    asked, 1-39
    bid, 1-39
    net, 1-36
    offering, mutual fund, 2-43
    redemption, bond, 1-21
    mutual fund, 2-104
    settlement, 1-45
Price averages, stock, 1-27
Price earnings ratio, 1-146
Price index, consumer, 1-117
Price indexes, stock, 1-131
Price make-up sheet,
    mutual fund, 2-85
Price ratio, 1-159
Primary distribution, 1-30
Prime paper, 1-4
Principal,
    NASD, 1-189
    conservation of as mutual
        fund objective, 2-32
    dealer as, 1-37
    employer as, 2-26
    registration of, NASD, 1-189
Principal types of investments,
    features of, 1-10
Principal underwriter, 1-32
    mutual fund, 2-78
Prior lien bonds, 1-19
Prior preferred stock, 1-16
Private offering, 1-34
Private placement, 1-33
Privileges, bond conversion, 1-181
Procedure,
    exchange type funds, exchange, 2-48
    large block, NYSE, 1-54
Production by divisions, 1-161
Production in units, 1-161

Profit,
    operating, 1-156
    underwriting, insurance
        companies, 1-173
Profit margin ratio, 1-158
Profitability ratio, 1-158
Property,
    improved, 1-7
    real, 1-6
Property dividend, 1-147
Property taxes, 2-18
Proprietorship, 1-4, 1-7, 1-10
Prospectus, 1-33, 1-83, 1-149
Prospectus,
    contractual plan, 2-120
    effective (final), 1-35
    information required in, 1-84
    mutual fund, 2-67
    red herring, 1-35
Provision for Federal and state
    income taxes, 1-157
Provisions of callable bond, 1-182
    of Investment Act of 1933, 1-81
    of Investment Company Act
        of 1940, 2-54
    of Securities Exchange Act
        of 1934, 1-87
Proxy, 1-14
Proxy fight, 1-14
Proxy statement, 1-15
Prudent Man Rule, 1-98
Public utilities, 1-161
    balance sheet analysis, 1-170
    financial position, 1-171
    income statement, 1-170
    operating profit ratio, 1-171
    regulation and rates, 1-170
Published material on mutual funds,
    use of, 2-112
Purchase, specialist block, 1-55
Purchase group, 1-32
Purchase of shares of mutual fund, 2-35
Purchasing power, 2-4
Purpose of life insurance, 2-2
Put, 1-68

Q

Qualifications for branch manager,
    NYSE, 1-191
    mutual fund custodian, 2-59
    registered representative,
        NASD, 1-187
    registered representative,
        NYSE, 1-189

Quotations,
 interdealer, 1-39
 newspaper, bond, 1-42
 newspaper, mutual fund, 1-41
 newspaper, NYSE listed
  stocks, 1-59
 newspaper, over-the-counter
  stocks, 1-39
 wholesale, 1-39

R

Railroads,
 analysis of, 1-166
 financial position, 1-168
Rate, bond interest, 1-181
Rate, of return, mutual fund, 2-96
Rates, regulation and,
 public utilities, 1-170
Rating, bond, 1-181
Ratio(s):
 book value per share, 1-157
 common stock, 1-158
 coverage of contingent
  interest, 1-167
 coverage of fixed charges, 1-167
 coverage of preferred
  dividends, 1-167
 current, 1-160
 debt-equity, 1-159
 debt to property, municipal
  bonds, 1-185
 dividend payout, 1-159
 earnings, 1-158
 earnings per share of
  common, 1-167
 earnings to fixed charges, 1-180
 expense, insurance
  companies, 1-173
 financial, 1-167
 fixed assets to net worth, 1-160
 growth, 1-159
 inventory turnover, 1-160
 loss, insurance companies, 1-173
 loss and expense,
  insurance companies, 1-173
 maintenance, railroads, 1-167
 municipal bonds, 1-185
 net quick assets to current
  liabilities, 1-161
 operating, railroads, 1-167
 operating profit,
  public utilities, 1-171
 price, 1-159
 price earnings, 1-146

 profit margin, 1-158
 profitability, 1-158
 sales, 1-158
 sales to net working capital, 1-168
 stability, 1-167
 transportation, railroads, 1-167
 underwriting profit, 1-173
 working capital, 1-158
 working capital per share, 1-158
Ratio analysis, 1-158
Reaction to news, market, 1-137
Real estate as
 an investment, 1-4, 1-7, 1-10
Real estate as a speculation, 1-3
Real estate investment
 trusts, 1-6, 2-11, 2-13
Real estate syndicate, 1-6, 2-11
Real property, 1-6
Recapitalization, 1-177
Receipt, constructive, 2-38
Receivable, accounts and
 notes, 1-151, 1-152
Receivers' certificates, 1-22
Recessions, 1-114
Record date, 1-46
Red herring prospectus, 1-35
Redemption,
 exchange-type funds, 2-50
 investment company shares, 2-77
 right of, investment company, 2-60
Redemption price, 1-17, 1-21
Redemption value, mutual fund
 shares, 2-104
Refinancing, 1-177
Refunding bond, 1-21
Reg A, 1-34
Registered bond, 1-21
Registered representative,
 NASD, requirements for, 1-187
 NASD, supervision of, 1-189
 NYSE, definition of, 1-190
 NYSE, requirements for, 1-189
 NYSE, supervision of, 1-191
Registered representative and
 customer, 2-25
 as agent, 2-26
Registered securities, 1-194
Registrants, joint, 2-22
Registrar, 1-13, 1-43
Registration,
 broker/dealer, 1-37
 grounds for denial of, 1-93
 NYSE, full and limited, 1-191
Registration and regulation, 1-80
 of principals, NASD, 1-189
 of securities, 2-21

Registration and Regulation—
     (Continued)
     of securities for:
          administrator, 2-25
          association, 2-25
Registration of securities for:
     corporation, 2-25
     executor, 2-25
     guardian, 2-24
     individual, 2-22
     partnership, 2-25
     pension or
          profit sharing trust, 2-25
     tax-exempt organization, 2-25
     trust, 2-24
Registration requirement, security, 1-83
Registration statement, 1-149
Regular way delayed delivery,
     NYSE, 1-70
Regular way delivery, NASD, 1-42
     NYSE, 1-70
Regulated investment companies, 2-37
Regulation A, 1-34
Regulation and rates,
     public utilities, 1-170
Regulation and registration, 1-80
Regulations T and U, 2-26
Reinvestment plan, mutual fund
     dividend, 2-35, 2-80
Reorganization, 1-176
Reports, investment company
     periodic, 2-62
Repurchase, investment company
     shares, 2-77
Required reserve, 1-107
Requirements,
     margin, 1-198
     registered representative,
          NASD, 1-187
     registered representative,
          NYSE, 1-189
     reserve, 1-111, 1-112
Reserve,
     life insurance cash, 1-5
     required, 1-107
Reserve Board, Federal, 1-111
Reserve requirement, 1-111, 1-112
Reserves, 1-152, 1-154, 1-162
Reserves for contingencies, 1-162
Resistance area, 1-139
Restricted management type
     mutual funds, 2-34
Restricted stock, 1-14
Restrictions, mutual fund policies
     and, 2-71
Retained earnings, 1-155
Return, 1-146

Return, mutual fund,
     misrepresenting, 2-100
     percentage, 2-97
     rate of, 2-97
Revenue bond, 1-20, 1-184
Reverse stock split, 1-177
Right(s):, 2-123
     and privileges, contractual plan and
          warrants, evaluation of, 1-178
     of accumulation, mutual funds, 2-37
     of inspection, stockholder's, 1-15
     of redemption, mutual funds, 2-60
     stock, 1-18
     stockholders', 1-13
     stockholders' liquidation, 1-14
     stockholders' pre-emptive, 1-15
     stockholders' transfer, 1-14
     stockholders' voting, 1-14
     subscription, 1-18
     survivorship, 2-22
Risk, 1-158
Risk, senior securities, 1-159
Round-lot unit of trading, 1-52
Rounding, 1-151
Rule, Prudent Man, 1-98

S

Sale, round-lot effective, 1-64
     wash, 1-91
Sales as income statement item, 1-156
Sales, break-point, mutual fund, 2-73
     short, 1-66
Sales charge, mutual fund, 2-36, 2-43
     mutual fund, limit on, 2-78
     mutual fund, literature
          requirement, 2-111
Sales literature, mutual fund, 2-94
Sales ratio, 1-158
Sales to net working capital ratio, 1-160
Savings accounts in banks, 1-3, 1-4, 1-10
Savings and loan account dividends, 1-5
Savings and loan share accounts, 1-4,
     1-5, 1-10
Savings bonds, E & H, 1-22
Scale order, 1-64
Schedule of investments (portfolio), 2-83
Seasonal changes, economic, 1-118
Seasonal movements, 1-137
SEC index, 1-132
SEC Statement of Policy, 2-93
Secondary capital market, 1-109
Secondary distributions, 1-30
     over-the-counter, 1-35
     New York Stock Exchange, 1-59
Secular changes, economic, 1-118
Secured bond, 1-19

INDEX

Securities, 1-1
    classes of corporate, 1-15
    corporate, 1-11
    customers', 1-75
    equity, 1-89
    exempted, 1-82
    foreign, 1-24
    fungible, 1-76
    Government, 1-183
    guaranteed, 1-183
    industrial, 1-171
    listed and unlisted, 1-42
    municipal, 1-4, 1-23, 1-184
    nature of, 1-11
    registered and unregistered, 1-194
    registration of, 2-21
    segregation of, 1-75
    senior corporate, 1-179
    when issued, 1-73
Securities Act of 1933, 1-81
Securities analysis, 1-126, 1-145
    industry approach, 1-165
Securities association, national, 1-99
Securities Exchange Act of 1934, 1-87
Securities transactions, 1-36
Securities underwriter, 1-31
Securities underwriting, 1-30
Security options, 1-66
Security position, 1-37
Security registration requirement, 1-83
Security values and taxes, 1-179
Segregation, bulk, 1-76
Segregation of securities, 1-75
Self-employed Individuals Tax
    Retirement Act, 2-14
Seller's option, NASD, 1-43
    NYSE, 1-70
Selling against the box, 1-67
Selling and administrative expense 1-156
Selling climax, 1-136
Selling group, 1-32
Selling short, 1-66
Senior charges, coverage of, 1-159
Senior mortgage bond, 1-19
Senior securities, corporate, 1-179
Serial bond, 1-21
Series bond, 1-21
Settlement, trading and, NASD, 1-46
Settlement date, 1-46
Settlement price, 1-45
Share accounts, savings and loan, 1-4,
    1-5, 1-10
Share value, changes in mutual
    fund, 2-74
Shareholders, mutual fund, 2-41
Shareholders, mutual fund, tax
    liability, 2-38

Shares, capital and income, leveraged
    fund, 2-6
    mutual fund, purchase of, 2-35
Sheets, green, pink and white, 1-37
Short interest, 1-136
Short sales, 1-66
Short sales by investment
    companies, 2-58
Short selling, 1-66
Short-term bond, 1-19
Short-term changes, economic, 1-121
Signature guarantee, 1-44
Silent partner, 1-8
Sinking fund bond, 1-21
Situations, special, 1-2, 1-176
Size, investment company, 2-58
Small Business Investment Companies,
    1-4, 1-8
Sole proprietorship, 1-4, 1-7, 1-10
Sources of financial information, 1-148
Special offering or bed, NYSE, 1-57
Special situations, 1-2, 1-176
Specialist, stock exchange, 1-51
Specialist block purchase or sale,
    NYSE, 1-55
Specialist's account, 1-193
Specialist's book, 1-51
Speculation and investment, 1-1
Spending, Government, 1-120
Spin-off, 1-147
Split-coupon bond, 1-20
Splits, stock, 1-177
Sponsor, 2-45
Spread (between bid and offer), 1-37,
    1-40
    (option), 1-68
    (underwriting), 1-31
Stability of capital as a mutual fund ob-
    jective, 2-32
Stability ratios, 1-159
Stabilization, 1-34
Standard & Poor's index, 1-131
Standby underwriting, 1-33
State obligations, 1-23, 1-184
Statement, income, 1-150, 1-155
    registration, 1-149
Statement of income and expense, mu-
    tual fund, 2-87
Statement of Policy, SEC, 2-93
Statements, corporate financial, 1-150
    mutual fund financial, 2-82
Statutory voting, 1-15
Stock:
    authorized, 1-17
    bank, 1-172
    callable preferred, 1-17
    capital, 1-16

Stock—(Continued)
common, 1-16
convertible preferred, 1-17
corporate, 1-4, 1-8, 1-10, 1-13, 1-15, 1-16
cumulative preferred, 1-16
dividends on, 1-14
growth, 1-159, 1-175
guaranteed, 1-17
income, 1-175
non-cumulative preferred, 1-16
outstanding, 1-18
participating preferred, 1-16
preferred, 1-16
preferred, analysis of, 1-182
prior preferred, 1-16
restricted, 1-14
technical analysis of individual, 1-137
treasury, 1-18
Stock ahead, 1-53
Stock analysis, factors in individual, 1-174
Stock average, 1-126
constant divisor and multiplier, 1-127
Stock certificate, 1-13
Stock clearing, over-the-counter, 1-44
Stock Clearing Corporation (NYSE), 1-71
Stock dividend, 1-147
Stock exchange (also see New York Stock Exchange), 1-29, 1-49
Stock exchange commissions, 1-64
Stock exchange floor members, 1-52
Stock fund (mutual), 2-34
Stock groupings, 1-127
Stock index, 1-126
Stock inventorying, 1-37
Stock power, 1-43, 1-75
Stock price averages, 1-127
Stock price indexes, 1-131
Stock quotations, 1-60
Stock right, 1-18, 1-69, 1-178
Stock split, 1-177
Stock split, reverse, 1-177
Stock ticker, 1-53
Stock transfer, 1-71
Stock yield, 1-147
Stockholders' equity, 1-152
Stockholders' rights, 1-13
Stop limit order, 1-62
Stop order, 1-62
Straddle, 1-68
Strap, 1-68
Street name, 1-75
Strip, 1-68

Structure, capital, 1-158
Subject market, 1-46
Subscription accounts, 1-193
Subscription right, 1-18
Supervision of accounts, 1-192
Supervision of registered representatives,
NASD, 1-189
NYSE, 1-191
Supervisory Jurisdiction, Office of, 1-189
Support level, 1-139
Surety bond, 1-72
Surplus, capital and earned, 1-152
Survivorship, joint tenants with right of, 2-22
Switch order, 1-64
Switching, mutual funds, 2-111
Syndicate, real estate, 1-6, 2-11
underwriting, 1-32
Syndicate manager, 1-32
Systematic investing plan, mutual fund, 2-81

T

Table, annuity, 2-8
Take time order, 1-63
Tape reading, 1-137
Tax, interest equalization, 1-24
Tax anticipation notes, 1-24, 1-108
Tax authority, 1-184
Tax districts, 1-184
Tax-exempt organizations, registration of securities for, 2-25
Tax liability, mutual fund shareholder's, 2-38
Tax loss, to establish, 2-17
Tax status of contractual plans, 2-127
municipal bonds, 1-185
Taxes, corporate, 2-18
estate and inheritance, 2-19
exchange-type funds, 2-50
gift, 2-20
income, 2-15
intangible property, 2-18
real property, 2-18
Taxes and mutual funds, 2-37
Taxes and security values, 1-179
Taxes payable, 1-152, 1-154
Technical analysis, 1-137
Technical analysis of individual stocks, 1-137
Technical factors in market analysis, 1-135
Tenants, joint, with right of survivorship, 2-22
Tenants by the entirety, 2-21

Tenants in common, 2-24
Termination of contractual plan, 2-124
Test, the acid, 1-161
Testamentary trust, registration of securities for, 2-24
Theory, Dow, 1-132
Theory of annuity, 2-7
Third market, 1-29
Ticker, stock, 1-53
Time order, 1-64
Tools of market analysis, 1-126
Total assets, 1-152, 1-153
Trade, cash, 1-46
Trade date, 1-46
Traded flat, 1-46
Trading and settlement, 1-46
Trading post, 1-51, 1-53
Transactions, exempted, 1-82
    fraudulent, 1-85
Transactions in securities, 1-36, 1-37
Transfer, stock, 1-71
    stockholder's right of, 1-14
Transfer agent, 1-13, 1-43
    mutual fund, 2-46
Transportation ratio, 1-167
Treasury bills, 1-6, 1-22
Treasury bonds, 1-4, 1-6, 1-10, 1-22
Treasury notes, 1-6, 1-22
Treasury obligations, 1-183
Treasury stock, 1-18
Trends, economic, 1-106, 1-114
    population, 1-120
Trust, deed of, 1-19
    indenture of, 1-19
    mutual fund as a, 2-46
    real estate investment, 2-11
Trust certificate, equipment, 1-22
    voting, 1-18
Trust Indenture Act, 1-182
Trusts, registration of securities for, 2-24
Two-dollar broker, 1-52
Types of investments, 1-3
Types of markets, 1-29

U

Unauthorized practice of law, 2-26
Underwriter, managing, 1-32
    mutual fund principal, 2-78
    principal, 1-32
    securities, 1-31
Underwriter's fee, mutual fund, 2-45
Underwriters, agreements among, 1-32
Underwriting, all or nothing, 1-32
    best efforts, 1-32
    standby, 1-33
Underwriting, 1-31

Underwriting agreement, 1-32
Underwriting commissions, 1-31
Underwriting contracts, mutual fund, 2-58
Underwriting discounts, 1-31
Underwriting group, 1-32
Underwriting markup, 1-31
Underwriting profit, insurance companies, 1-173
Underwriting securities, 1-30
Underwriting spread, 1-31
Underwriting syndicate, 1-32
Uniform Commercial Code, 1-73
Uniform Gifts to Minors Act, 2-21
Units, variable annuity, 2-10
Unlimited tax bonds, 1-23
Unlisted securities, 1-42
Unregistered securities, 1-194
Use of published material on mutual funds, 2-112
Utilities, public, balance sheet analysis, 1-170
    financial position, 1-171
    income statement analysis, 1-170
    operating profit ratio, 1-171
    regulation and rates, 1-170

V

Valuation approach, 1-145
Valuation of rights and warrants, 1-178
Value, book, 1-147, 1-153
    cash surrender, 1-5, 1-10
    market, 1-147
    net asset, mutual fund, 2-43
    par, 1-147
Values and taxes, securities, 1-179
Variable annuities, 2-7
    comparison with mutual funds, 2-13
Variable annuity concept, 2-9
Variable annuity units, 2-10
Variable ratio formula, 1-143
Venture, joint, 1-8
Voluntary plan, mutual fund, 2-81
Volume, 1-136
Voting, cumulative, 1-15
    non-cumulative, 1-15
    statutory, 1-15
Voting rights, stockholders', 1-14
Voting trust certificates, 1-18

W

Warrant, 1-18
Warrants, valuation of rights and, 1-178

INDEX

Wash sale, 1-91
When, as, and if, 1-36
When issued securities, 1-73
Wholesale quotations, 1-39
Withdrawal plans, mutual fund, 2-35,
    2-82, 2-133
Working capital ratio, 1-158
Workout market, 1-46
World Bank, 1-123
Working capital per share, 1-158

Y

Yield,
    bond and stock, 1-147
    to maturity, 1-148